INDIANAPOLIS
HOCKEY

INDIANAPOLIS CAPITALS
AMERICAN HOCKEY LEAGUE CHAMPIONS
1949-1950

The 1949-50 Indianapolis Capitals became the first team in American Hockey League history to win the Calder Cup championship. Led by goaltender Terry Sawchuk, AHL career scoring leader Fred Glover and longtime players Enio Scilisizzi, Al Dewsbury, Nels Podolsky, Don Morrison, Rod Morrison and coach Ott Heller, the Capitals became one of the AHL's all-time great teams. Throughout their run from 1939 to 1952, the Capitals supplied the Detroit Red Wings with players, and formed the foundation of the Wings' early 1950s dynasty. The players in this photo, from left to right, are: (front row) Sawchuk, Podolsky, Don Morrison, Heller, Pat Lundy, Rod Morrison, and Ross "Lefty" Wilson; (second row) Scilisizzi, Benny Woit, Dewsbury, Joe Lund, Max Quackenbush, Clare Raglan, and Gerry Reid; and (back row) Gordon Haidy, Jim Uniac, Glover, Doug McKay, and Lyall Wiseman. (Courtesy of the Blaise Lamphier collection.)

INDIANAPOLIS
HOCKEY

Andrew Smith

ARCADIA

Copyright © 2004 by Andrew Smith
ISBN 0-7385-3336-X

Published by Arcadia Publishing
Charleston SC, Chicago IL, Portsmouth NH, San Francisco CA

Printed in Great Britain

Library of Congress Catalog Card Number: 2004110783

For all general information contact Arcadia Publishing at:
Telephone 843-853-2070
Fax 843-853-0044
E-mail sales@arcadiapublishing.com
For customer service and orders:
Toll-Free 1-888-313-2665

Visit us on the internet at http://www.arcadiapublishing.com

The entrance to the Indiana State Fairgrounds and the ticket window points the way to the Fairgrounds Coliseum, where the Indianapolis Capitals played hockey, in 1949. Fans would pass through this gate en route to the rink. The Coliseum—later renamed the Pepsi Coliseum—has been a major part of Indianapolis hockey since it was built in 1939. (Courtesy of Indiana State Fairgrounds.)

CONTENTS

ACKNOWLEDGMENTS

First and foremost, I would like to thank my wife Anne, who made this dream hers, encouraged me during long hours of research; and supported me throughout the process of putting together this book; and I thank God for giving me the vision and diligence to do such a project.

I would like to thank Jason Burkman of the Indianapolis Ice and Andy Klotz of the Indiana State Fairgrounds, who were very helpful in supplying images and several other pieces of information for this book. Thanks also to Al Josey, Rusty Lovell, Paul O'Neill, Jacob Spade, Judy Stuart, and the many others who provided photographs and other information for this book.

Thanks go to the staff at the Indianapolis-Marion County Public Library's microfilm room, who were so helpful during hours of research. Ralph Slate, your work on hockeydb.com has helped put players' names and statistics to historic teams everywhere, and inspired me to find the faces and the stories behind those numbers in my hometown. Thanks to Marc Foster and to the Hockey Research Association, which has provided me webspace to maintain this history on-line and immeasurable help in tracking down numbers and stats. To Jeff Ruetsche at Arcadia Publishing, who helped make this a reality.

And thanks go to my parents, for taking me to the Coliseum and Market Square Arena on winter nights when I was young and introducing me to this wonderful game, and to my many friends who enjoy spending winter evenings watching hockey.

And to all of you, the readers, for having an interest in Indianapolis hockey.

INTRODUCTION

In the middle of the Indiana cornfields lies Indianapolis, a place best known for its generations-old devotion to basketball and auto racing. As the United States was exiting the Depression, minor league hockey was growing throughout the Upper Midwest and the populace was looking for new ways to spend its entertainment dollar.

In that environment, the city of Indianapolis was given a new winter diversion and a new set of heroes to add to the legends made in the high school basketball tournament a few miles west at Butler Fieldhouse, and the ones created by the Indianapolis Motor Speedway even farther west.

In the fall of 1939, hockey came to Indianapolis in the form of the Indianapolis Capitals, beginning a tradition that would continue—on and off—up into the present. Those early years were marked by curiosity. The first television broadcast was still a few years away, so most Indianapolis residents had never seen a hockey game.

That didn't stop them from turning out. An overflow crowd of 9,193 fans showed up for the first game—a 5-1 victory over the Syracuse Stars November 10, 1939—and they kept coming back for many years.

With the exception of four and a half years in the 1970s when the World Hockey Association's Indianapolis Racers captured Central Indiana's fancy, Indianapolis has always been a minor-league market. It has housed teams at various levels, one step below the NHL and lower; these are the more entertainment-oriented levels of professional hockey. Like many minor-league cities, the hockey scene in Indianapolis has experienced flux. From the 13-year run of the Indianapolis Capitals that many among the 10,000-fan throngs of the late 1940s figured would never end, through the brief one-month run of the Indianapolis Capitols in 1963, when the team was forced to move after the Fairgrounds Coliseum explosion, to the eras of the Checkers and Ice, each of which spent their tenures in two different leagues, Indianapolis hockey has weathered the changes.

Those many hockey teams carved out their own niche among the growing sports scene in Indianapolis with loyal, even rabid, fan bases. The market became more crowded in 1967 with the arrival of the Indiana Pacers, and again in 1984 with the Indianapolis Colts, and again in the 1990s with the addition of NASCAR and Formula One races at the Indianapolis Motor Speedway. These other sporting contenders might have overshadowed hockey at times, but Indy remains a solid hockey town.

Teams came and went as society changed. After 1939, television came along, and was a big reason for the rapid demise of many minor-league teams in the 1950s—including the Caps. By the late 1950s, the Indianapolis Chiefs were televising some of their games. The interstate highway system was built and teams switched from train travel, preferred in the 1940s, to using buses in the 1950s, to cross-country airplane flights in the 1970s and '80s. As the Indianapolis Checkers and Ice played through the last 20 years of the 20th Century, cable television brought hockey into every living room, which created new fans, but also new competition for the local hockey teams. With each larger change in society, so did the approach of minor league hockey change—to a point where, by the 1990s, the Indianapolis Ice were as well-known for their innovative promotional ideas as for the game they played.

But through it all, Indianapolis' position in the hockey world has been a unique one: local fans have gotten a chance to see NHL stars many years before they become Hall of Famers. Terry Sawchuk, a man who has been considered the greatest goaltender of all time, spent two of his formative seasons backstopping the Indianapolis Capitals, leading them to a championship in 1950. Two other Hall of Famers—Harry Lumley and Glenn Hall—also played goal for the Caps. Four decades later, Dominik Hasek did the same for the Indianapolis Ice. A number of other hockey greats—from Sid Abel to Marcel Pronovost to Alex Delvecchio to Herb Lewis—passed through Indy. So did longtime hockey executives Max McNab, Tommy Ivan, Jim Devellano, and Hockey News publisher Ken McKenzie.

Wayne Gretzky and Mark Messier began their big-league careers as members of the Indianapolis Racers. Dave Keon played the end of his Hall of Fame career with the same team. Joe Turner—the man for whom the International Hockey League named the Turner Cup—led the Indianapolis Caps to their first championship in 1942, before perishing in World War II. Twice, the Turner Cup spent a summer in Indianapolis.

As a hockey market, Indy created its own legends—Herbie Lewis, Hal Jackson, Cliff Simpson, and Enio Scilisizzi weren't household names in national hockey in the 1940s, but they were in the Circle City. The same goes for Pierre Brillant and Cliff Hicks in the 1950s; Kevin Devine, Garth MacGuigan, and Darcy Regier in the 1980s; Sean Williams and Jimmy Waite in the 1990s; and Bernie John and Jamie Morris as the 21st century began. Seven different Indianapolis teams have celebrated professional hockey championships from 1942 to 2000.

While the love affair between the core local fans and their hockey players has long been great, never was it more intense than in the mid-1970s, when the WHA's Indianapolis Racers brought big-time hockey to Indy. Indianapolis was hungry for a winner, and sellout crowds showed their support in the big games of 1976 and '77 when the Racers made the playoffs. Pat "Whitey" Stapleton, Ken Block, Kim Clarkson, Andy Brown, Michel Dion, Hugh Harris, and Brian McDonald became household names, and the Racers were the toast of the town—even out drawing the ABA's Indiana Pacers in the 1975–76 season. When the Racers lost their final playoff game in 1976, fans gave them a standing ovation despite a 6-0 deficit on the scoreboard. A year later, the crowd roared in celebration when the Racers swept the Cincinnati Stingers at Market Square Arena.

Indianapolis hockey is the players—those who went on to become legends and those who stayed put and became fan favorites. It is the fans—the ones who have supported eight different teams through four buildings and five different leagues, the ones who were standing on their seats and making the Coliseum's rafters shake when the final seconds ticked down in the 1990 championship. Indy hockey is the old green wooden seats in the boxes at the Fairgrounds Coliseum, the Superfans sitting in the rafters at Market Square Arena. It is Gene Peacosh's goal, Andy Brown's maskless face, Herb Lewis' rapport with the fans, and Ray LeBlanc's red, white and blue mask. It is a tapestry of eras, teams, and memories.

It is a tradition.

ONE
The Beginning
CAPITALS 1939–1945

In the winter of 1939, Indianapolis was known worldwide for one thing—the Indianapolis 500-Mile Race, which was preparing for its 27th installment that spring. And the state of Indiana was known not only for racing, but for its love of basketball—particularly the high school variety.

But Arthur Wirtz had a dream for the city that made legends of Wilbur Shaw and Johnny Wooden. He was going to build a building and bring a new game to Indianapolis sport fans.

That winter, Works Progress Administration workers began pouring Hoosier limestone into a site on the southern end of the Indiana State Fairgrounds where an old wooden Coliseum had stood and a few steps away from one of the nation's top one-mile dirt racetracks. Wirtz, who managed figure skating legend Sonja Henie at the time, would manage the $1,000,000 Coliseum when it was finished.

When the final strokes of maroon paint were applied to the walls ringing the arena floor, a new sport was brought to town—hockey.

The International-American Hockey League—soon to drop the "International" from its name—was expanding into the Upper Midwest. Wirtz used Henie as a carrot to get the IAHL to place a team in his new showplace in Indiana, and the Indianapolis Capitals were born, playing their first game in the fall of 1939.

Herb Lewis, a man known as the fastest skating defenseman in hockey throughout the 1930s, was hired to be a player-coach and to introduce this new game to Hoosiers. The Detroit Red Wings would provide players, making Indianapolis their top farm club—a relationship that would last 13 years.

Indianapolis hockey actually began in Hershey, Pennsylvania, where the Caps beat the Bears 4-3 in their inaugural game.

Two nights later, on November 2, they headed to the 8,000-seat Coliseum, where overflow seating was installed to handle a crowd of 9,193 curious citizens who paid 40 and 75 cents to witness the 8:30 p.m. debut of hockey in the city, a game pitting the Capitals against Syracuse Stars. The mayor showed up. So did the governor, lieutenant governor, Red Wings president Jack Adams, and IAHL president Maurice Podoloff. Announcer Bob Elson came down from

Chicago to explain the new game to the fans.

The debut was a success. William Fox of the *Indianapolis News* said, "Indianapolis, well 9,193 of us, took to ice hockey last night like father to Junior's first electric train."

Don Deacon scored the first goal 9:35 into the game, and Bill Hudson scored two more, sending the Capitals to a 5-1 win. Two nights later, the Caps beat Philadelphia 2-0 in front of 6,053 fans on a Sunday night. For nearly two decades after, Sundays were the traditional hockey night in Indianapolis: the Caps played at home at 8:30 p.m. nearly every winter Sunday night for the next 13 years.

The Caps won the Ted Oke Trophy as the West Division champion in their first season, facing East Division winner Providence in the opening round of the playoffs. Providence defenseman Harold "Hal" Jackson banked the puck into the net off goaltender Alfie Moore's stick after 42:23 of overtime to beat the Caps 2-1 in the opening game, setting the tone for a series Providence would eventually win 3-2—taking all three of its home games and winning the deciding tilt with a 2-0 score. The Reds went on to win the Calder Cup.

A year later, Jackson was dealt to Indianapolis and become the face of hockey in the city, going on from his playing days to become a fixture as an official and youth-league director for the next several decades.

The Caps spoiled the fan base with a championship-caliber team right off the bat. With several players having been called up to Detroit, including Hudson, their leading scorer, they stumbled to a 17-28-11 record in 1940-41. But they came back the next year with a memorable team, sporting a number of top players—among them veterans Connie Brown, Hec Kilrea, Les Douglas, Joe Fisher, John "Red" Keating, and bruising defensemen Buck Jones and Dick Behling. But the real hotshot was a 22-year-old goaltender with an impressive amateur record, Joe Turner, the first in a long line of legendary netminders to play in Indianapolis.

Turner made quite an impression in his debut against the Washington Lions, stopping every advance and making a second-period goal by Adam Brown stand up in a 1-0 victory. Turner wouldn't give up a goal until the third period of the Caps' second game, a 5-1 win in Pittsburgh. It was a preview of things to come, as the Caps won their last five games and rolled to the Western Division title with a 34-15-7 record. One of those games, a 2-0 victory in Buffalo, almost ended early, as the Bisons' fans pelted the ice with pennies after referee Rabbit McVeigh called a misconduct on Buffalo's Jack Toupin. McVeigh declared a forfeit, but later let the game resume and the Capitals held off their foes.

The division title meant the Caps would face former NHL legend Eddie Shore's Springfield Indians in the opening round of the playoffs. Shore's teams often exhibited their owner's toughness on the ice, and they were always a thorn in the side for the Caps, who took on the personality of their own coach and were known as one of the league's fastest-skating teams. The series lived up to its billing as an epic battle for victory.

Springfield won the first game 4-2 at the Fairgrounds behind a hat trick by Bill Summerhill; but Douglas did him one better, with three goals and an assist in Game 2, and the Caps won going away 10-3. Springfield got the upper hand in Game 3, winning 6-3, giving the Indians a chance to clinch the series at home. But the Caps rallied in the third period as Doug McCaig tied the game with a breakaway goal, and Gus Giesebrecht won it when he pushed a shot that hit both posts across the line to give the Caps a 4-3 victory.

The Caps' win set up a decisive Game 5 in Indianapolis, and another back-and-forth struggle was underway. Springfield's Gerry O'Flaherty tied it at 2-2 with 12 minutes to go, and the Indians began pelting Turner's net with shots. He kept the game tied going into overtime, and then made 14 stops in the first 19 minutes of OT. With the bigger Indians carrying the play, it appeared a matter of time before they scored the winner. Instead, McAtee turned in a spectacular play of his own. Springfield's Bob Dill was trying to bring the puck out of the defensive zone when McAtee swooped in, stripped the puck from his stick, and shoveled it into the Springfield net to give the Caps a 3-2 victory in both the game and the series and send them into the Calder Cup Finals.

Western Division rival Hershey would be the Capitals' opponent in the finals. They'd split six regular-season games and finished three points apart in the standings. The series played out just like the one before—the two teams split 5-4 decisions in Indianapolis before heading to Hershey. The Caps rallied to win Game 3 2-1 on a shorthanded third-period goal by Keating. Hershey won Game 4 3-2 on a third-period goal by Wally Hergesheimer.

They headed back to Indianapolis for the decisive game, having played four one-goal thrillers, all but one of which had been decided in the final 20 minutes. The packed house of 8,867 might have expected a nail-biter, but fans got to celebrate early. Keating, Sandy Ross, and Joe Fisher scored three goals in a 51-second span in the first period, opening the floodgates to an 8-3 victory and the first hockey championship in Indianapolis.

The honors began to flow in—with 17 points each, Keating and Douglas became the AHL's career playoff scoring recordholders. The next night, coach Lewis was presented both the Ted Oke Trophy—symbolic of West Division supremacy—and the Calder Cup, in a reception at the Columbia Club. The players were given monogrammed travel bags at the reception. "This is the grandest bunch of kids I've ever had the pleasure of working with," Lewis told the crowd, as reported by the *Indianapolis Star*.

But signs that things were beginning to change were apparent as the players divided their shares and scattered. America joined World War II at mid-season, and several player left to join the war effort. Lewis went to work immediately in a shell-loading plant. Several joined the Canadian or American armed forces, including Turner, who would perish in combat in 1944. When the war ended, the founders of the new International Hockey League named their championship trophy for Turner. IHL champions hoisted the Turner Cup for the next 56 seasons.

The war drastically changed the game. The number of teams in the AHL dropped from 10 in 1941–42 to six in 1943–44. With the top NHL and AHL players in the service, many would-be Capitals who remained spent the war wearing Detroit Red Wings sweaters. Wartime travel restrictions severely cut into attendance. In 1942–43, the Capitals drew around 7,000 fans per game for Sunday night contests. When gas rationing began in December, the average dropped to 4,000. Of the championship team, Hal Jackson, Adam Brown, Joe Fisher, and Judd McAtee remained, but the rest of the squad was largely made up of rookies and minor-league veterans from elsewhere. One goaltender, Floyd Perras, played every minute in goal, and backstopped the Caps to a respectable 29-23-4 record. Brown shattered the Capitals' single-season scoring record with 34 goals and 85 points. The Caps had six eight-goal games that season.

The Caps advanced to the Calder Cup Finals again, sweeping Pittsburgh and Cleveland in the opening rounds. Old nemesis Eddie Shore was back, running the Buffalo Bisons this time around—Springfield had been shuttered for the war. And this time Shore got the upper hand: the Bisons won all three games.

Due to wartime player shortages, the Capitals were assigned a teenaged goaltender—18-year-old Harry Lumley—for the 1943–44 season. Lewis resigned his coaching position to work at an industrial job in Indianapolis. He was replaced with former Red Wing John Sorrell, who was described as a quiet, mild-mannered strategist. A new rule was put in place that was expected to help the speedy Capitals—the introduction of the center red line. It allowed players to pass the puck forward across their own blue line for the first time, opened up the game, increased scoring, and ushered in hockey's modern era.

However, the faster-skating game created a new headache for a rookie like Lumley, whose road to the Hockey Hall of Fame began with a 5-3 victory over Buffalo. The Caps started the year with a 2-7-6 record, but started to turn things around with the help of another teenager—18-year-old Vic Lynn, who scored twice in a 16-second span to beat Pittsburgh 5-3 in mid-December. Indianapolis rallied to finish 20-18-16 and finish second in the West Division, but lost to Buffalo 4-1 in a best-of-five series.

Lumley returned for the 1944–45 season and turned in a lot of steady play early, starting with a 2-1 victory over Buffalo in the season opener—although the Bisons took another wartime specialty, a between-periods relay race for $100 in war bonds. But when Lumley backstopped four straight wins to give the Caps a 10-6-5 record, he found himself in Detroit. Connie Dion replaced him in Indianapolis and led the team to a 25-24-4 mark. With the war nearing its end, crowds began to increase, creeping back up to the levels enjoyed before the hostilities began. The Caps clinched their fourth consecutive playoff spot on the last day of the regular season, beating Cleveland 8-4 behind four goals by Pete Leswick. The Hershey Bears ended the Caps' run in the semifinals, four games to one.

There was a new rival on the scene—the St. Louis Flyers had been birthed that season and sported a roster made up largely of ex-Capitals, including goaltender Jimmy Franks. With World War II ending, familiar faces were likely to return to Indianapolis along with the crowds that were also coming back. The first six years had set the stage for what would become the golden era of early Indianapolis hockey.

The inaugural Indianapolis Capitals pose in the Fairgrounds Coliseum before a game against the New Haven Eagles. Team members, from left to right, are: (front row) Bill Thomson, Connie Brown, Jimmy Franks, Archie Wilder, and Joe Carveth; (back row) unidentified staff, Ron Hudson, Joe Fisher, Buck Jones, Eddie Bush, Bob Whitelaw, Alex Motter, Byron McDonald, player/coach Herb Lewis, and general manager Dick Miller. (Courtesy of the Blaise Lamphier collection.)

HOCKEY ★ ★
★ ★ SCHEDULE
1939 - 1940
NEW COLOSSEUM
STATE FAIRGROUNDS

HEADQUARTERS FOR SPORTING EVENTS

Compliments of

INDIANA THEATRE MAGAZINE and NEWS SHOP

RILEY 5916
Home of News

Herbie Lewis
PLAYING MANAGER
CONGRATULATIONS !
We're Happy
To Have You
With Us.

OUR INVITATION COME IN AND BROWSE AROUND

INDIANA THEATRE
MAGAZINE and NEWS
SHOP - RI. 5916

This is the first-ever pocket schedule produced for a local hockey team. Much different than today's schedules, this one was apparently put out by the Indiana News Company. Note the spelling of the home rink— "New Colosseum."

INDIANA THEATRE MAGAZINE AND NEWS SHOP
134 WEST WASHINGTON STREET ‹ ‹ ◆ › › INDIANAPOLIS, INDIANA

Following is the season schedule of the Indianapolis professional hockey team:

INDIANAPOLIS AT HOME	INDIANAPOLIS ABROAD
Syracuse................Friday, Nov. 10	At Hershey........Saturday, Nov. 4
Philadelphia.........Sunday, Nov. 12	At Syracuse..........Sunday, Nov. 5
Providence.......Thursday, Nov. 16	At Pittsburgh....Saturday, Nov. 11
Cleveland.............Sunday, Nov. 19	At Cleveland.....Saturday, Nov. 18
New Haven........Thursday, Nov. 23	At Pittsburgh....Saturday, Nov. 25
Pittsburgh............Sunday, Nov. 26	At Springfield....Saturday, Dec. 2
Syracuse............Thursday, Nov. 30	At Providence......Sunday, Dec. 3
Cleveland............Thursday, Dec. 14	At Hershey.....Wednesday, Dec. 6
Hershey................Sunday, Dec. 17	At Philadelphia..Saturday, Dec. 9
Springfield ....Tuesday, Dec. 19	At New Haven......Sunday, Dec. 10
Cleveland.............Monday, Dec. 25	At Cleveland Saturday, Dec. 23
Pittsburgh...........Thursday, Jan. 4	At New Haven......Wed., Dec. 27
Philadelphia...........Sunday, Jan. 7	At Providence..Thursday, Dec. 28
New Haven........Thursday, Jan. 11	At Springfield....Saturday, Dec. 30
Hershey...........Thursday, Jan. 18	At Syracuse..........Sunday, Dec. 31
Pittsburgh............Sunday, Jan. 21	At Cleveland....Saturday, Jan. 6
Providence........Thursday, Jan. 25	At Syracuse.........Sunday, Jan. 14
Springfield...........Sunday, Jan. 28	At Pittsburgh....Saturday, Jan. 20
Syracuse..............Thursday, Feb. 1	At Philadelphia......Wed., Jan. 31
Cleveland............Sunday, Feb. 4	At Hershey..........Saturday, Feb. 3
New Haven..........Thursday, Feb. 8	At Cleveland......Saturday, Feb. 10
Hershey...........Sunday, Feb. 11	At Pittsburgh....Saturday, Feb. 17
Providence........Thursday, Feb. 15	At Providence......Sunday, Feb. 18
Philadelphia........Thursday, Feb. 29	At Philadelphia......Wed., Feb. 21
Pittsburgh............Thursday, Mar. 7	At Hershey......Thursday, Feb. 22
Springfield..........Sunday, Mar. 10	At Springfield....Saturday, Feb. 24
Syracuse............Thursday, Mar. 14	At New Haven....Sunday, Feb. 25
Hershey................Sunday, Mar. 17	At Syracuse....Wednesday, Feb. 28

◆ GREETING CARDS ◆ FOREIGN PUBLICATIONS ◆ NOVELTIES ◆
◆ RENTAL LIBRARY ◆ NEWSPAPERS FROM ALL OVER THE WORLD ◆
Indianapolis' Only Complete Magazine Shop

Pictured is the cover and the Capitals' lineup from a program for a 1940–41 game against the Pittsburgh Hornets. It was the Capitals' second season in American Hockey League play.

Jud McAtee scored the series-winning goal in overtime to beat the Springfield Indians in the first round of the 1942 Calder Cup Playoffs. Springfield had been buzzing the Capitals' net before McAtee forced a turnover in the defensive zone and scored to send the Caps to the Calder Cup Finals, where they eventually won the first of their two AHL championships. (Courtesy of the Indiana Historical Society/Bass Photo collection. Photo unnumbered.)

Bill Thomson, Byron "Bucko" McDonald and John Sorrell pose in the Coliseum during the 1943–44 season. Thomson played 214 games with the Capitals in two different stints between 1939 and 1945 and was their leading scorer with 58 points in 1943–44. He totaled 187 points during that span. McDonald totaled 93 points in 95 games between 1939 and 1944. Sorrell was the Capitals' second coach, brought in to replace Herb Lewis in 1943. He coached the Capitals for two and a half seasons, taking the team to the AHL playoffs each year. He also totaled 80 points in 107 games as a player during that span. (Courtesy of the Indiana Historical Society/ Bass Photo collection #263236F-3.)

Jake Forbes, Harry Lumley, and "Red" Kane pose in front of the goals at the Coliseum during the 1943–44 season. Lumley made his professional debut with the Capitals and played 76 games in Indianapolis, posting a 2.64 goals against average, and jump-starting a career that led him to the Hockey Hall of Fame. Forbes and Kane each played parts of two seasons with the Capitals as defensemen. (Courtesy of the Indiana Historical Society/Bass Photo collection #263236F-1.)

Jack Hewson, Dick Kowcinak and Tony Bukovich in the Coliseum during the 1944–45 season. It was the final year of wartime hockey. Bukovich played four years with the Caps, totaling 137 points between 1943 and 1947. Kowcinak totaled 75 points in 84 games from 1943 to 1945, while Hewson joined the team in 1944 and played two seasons in Indianapolis. (Courtesy of the Indiana Historical Society/Bass Photo collection #263236F-5.)

Two

The Golden Era

Capitals 1945–1952

In the fall of 1945, things couldn't get much better in North America. American and Canadian soldiers triumphantly came home after victory in Europe and Japan. Prosperity returned with the soldiers who came back with their war paychecks, while their wives had collected them in war industries back home. Rationing was over, and people were buying cars and driving them again, and looking for a good time.

For the same reasons, the fortunes of the hockey world were on the upswing as well. The player shortages of the previous three seasons were a thing of the past and teams began to stock their rosters with the familiar faces of those who had left the sport to join the service. Teams that had shortages now had abundance. Lower-level minor leagues were resurrected. The AHL grew to its prewar size of eight teams. The postwar years ushered in what would be the golden era in American professional sports.

The Capitals benefited greatly from the influx of returning servicemen. High-scoring centers Les Douglas and Gerry Brown were back. So were left wing Carl "Winky" Smith, right wing Roy Sawyer, and defenseman Sandy Ross. Another Canadian Army vet was slated for duty, defenseman Andy Branigan, who had played in the NHL's Brooklyn Americans prior to the war. Floyd Perras, who was the Caps' starting goaltender in 1942–43, one of several goalies vying for the job in nets, began the season in goal. The most obvious signs of the war's end came in the crowds—nearly 9,000 showed up in Buffalo to see the Caps beat their Bisons in the season opener 3-2. The next night, 8,728 fans filled the Coliseum to see the Caps tie the Bisons 3-3.

Tom Wilson replaced Perras in goal at midseason, but the winning went on. In his AHL debut, Wilson faced only 10 shots against Providence; he stopped them all,, and the Caps scored eight goals. The Caps started 14-6-4, but a 1-5-1 stretch ended Johnny Sorrell's coaching tenure and brought Earl Seibert to the helm. Wilson made the transition memorable, blanking Cleveland 9-0 in Sorrell's final game, shutting out Pittsburgh and Providence in the next two games, and putting together a 217:34 shutout streak.

The Capitals won their third Ted Oke Trophy as division champions with a 33-20-9 record, and Les Douglas led the AHL in scoring with 90 points. Pete Leswick and defenseman Hugh Millar were named All-Stars. Their reward was a date with Buffalo, winners of the Eastern

Division with an AHL-record of 84 points. The Bisons won four of the five games and went on to win the Calder Cup.

As the 1946–47 season opened, it became evident the AHL's balance of power was shifting to the west, where the largest markets resided—Cleveland, Indianapolis, St. Louis, and Pittsburgh. Defending champion Buffalo also moved to the western division. The stage was set for one of the wildest playoff chases in hockey history—five first-line teams vying for three spots. The Capitals had a new coach, Tommy Ivan, but flew to a 33-18-13 record, numbers nearly identical to the division-winning mark of the year before. More than half the roster was new, with players that would become familiar faces in the lineup—like Enio Scilisizzi, Don and Rod Morrison, Nels Podolsky, and Al Dewsbury. The Caps posted several lopsided wins over the weaker eastern teams—by scores of 10-0, 8-1, 14-2 and 8-3. After an 8-1 victory over the Philadelphia Rockets on November 2, a Philly writer said the AHL should simply hand the Calder Cup over to the Caps without further ado because they were such a good team. Little did the writer know that the Caps wouldn't even get a chance to play for the Cup.

The Caps struggled to win low-scoring battles against division foes. Crowds remained huge and seats were added to the Coliseum floor to expand capacity to 11,000. As the season wound down, the top four teams in the division were separated by four points. The Caps fell out of third as March rolled around, and the team needed to win both games in the final weekend. Instead they lost 13-1 to Hershey and fell out of the playoffs, one point behind third-place Pittsburgh. They had posted the best record of any hockey team to miss the playoffs. Les Douglas, Cliff Simpson, and Hugh Millar were named All-Stars, some consolation.

Ivan was promoted to the Red Wings for the 1947–48 season, and former Detroit goaltender Johnny Mowers replaced him as head coach. The rebuilt squad was called the fastest in the AHL and had little difficulty scoring, led by Cliff Simpson, who scored a team-record 110 points, including 12 goals and 10 assists in a six-game stretch late in the year. But second-year goaltender Red Almas and a young defense struggled to keep the puck out of the net. They finished at a respectable 32-30-6 mark, but well out of playoff contention.

Help was on the way in the form of a young prodigy with a crooked arm who was coming up from the USHL's Omaha Knights—Terry Sawchuk. Vezina Trophies and Stanley Cups were in his future, but in 1948, he was a 20-year-old rookie trying to unseat future Hall of Famer Harry Lumley in Detroit. The Capitals also had a new coach, Ott Heller, who taught Sawchuk the "gorilla crouch" he'd become well-known for in the NHL—he bent his 6-foot-2 frame low and forward so he could see oncoming shots while staying on his feet. In the days when goaltenders didn't wear masks, the crouch was hazardous, but it was also effective. Another rookie, Fred Glover—who spent the next two decades rewriting the AHL record books—came up from Omaha with Sawchuk. But they were trumped by fellow newcomer Gerry Reid who had a hat trick in the season opener. Sawchuk stopped 25 shots in the 5-1 Capitals victory over Buffalo.

It didn't take long for Sawchuk to shine. He gave up two or fewer goals eight times in the Caps' first 10 games. He recorded his first career shutout in St. Louis—but it ended up a 0-0 tie. The Capitals found themselves locked in a tight playoff race late in the year again, but things went amiss. Sawchuk was hurt, a pulled groin muscle. He went into the hospital, but he didn't miss a game until March 10 against New Haven, when he was hit by a puck in the face and collapsed. The season came down to one game against the Pittsburgh Hornets, with the winner going to the postseason and the loser staying home. Sawchuk was brilliant, stopping all but one shot. With 1:40 to go, Rod Morrison flung a rink-wide pass to brother Don, who scored to give the Caps a 2-1 victory, a 39-17-12 record, and a playoff bid. Sawchuk was named the league's rookie of the year. Sadly, their playoff run was short; the Hershey Bears, who had finished 29 points behind the Capitals in the standings, swept Indy 5-0 and 4-3 in the best-of-3 series.

The Capitals established themselves as one of the AHL's elite teams in 1949, but didn't have a championship to show for it. In 1950, they were out to prove they belonged. Sawchuk was back. So were Reid, Glover, Enio Scilisizzi, Nels Podolsky, the Morrison brothers, Gordon Haidy, and Al Dewsbury. The team struggled out of the gate, but an 8-0-4 streak put them back

P—Penalty   S—Shots | A—Assists   G—Goal

INDIANAPOLIS CAPITALS

LINE-UP

No.	Name	Position	ASSISTS	GOALS	TIME IN PENALTY BOX	NUMBER OF STOPS BY GOAL TENDER		
						1st Period	2nd Period	3rd Period
1.	TOM WILSON	Goal						
2.	DOUG McCAIG	Defense				--1----	--1----	--1---
3.	ROLLIE McLENAHAN	Defense				--2----	--2----	--2---
4.	HUGH MILLAR	Defense				--3----	--3----	--3---
5.	ANDY BRANIGAN	Defense				--4----	--4----	--4---
6.	GEORGE BLAKE	Left Wing				--5----	--5----	--5---
7.	LES DOUGLAS	Center				--6----	--6----	--6---
8.	FERNAND GAUTHIER	Left Wing				--7----	--7----	--7---
9.	JIMMY CONACHER	Left Wing				--8----	--8----	--8---
10.	TONY BUKOVITCH	Center				--9----	--9----	--9---
11.	JOHNNY HOLOTA	Center				--10----	--10----	--10---
12.	STEVE WOCHY	Right Wing				--11----	--11----	--11---
14.	CLIFF SIMPSON	Right Wing				--12----	--12----	--12---
16.	PETE LESWICK	Right Wing				--13----	--13----	--13---
17.	JERRY BROWN	Center				--14----	--14----	--14---
	EARL SIEBERT	Defense				--15----	--15----	--15---
						--16----	--16----	--16---
						--17----	--17----	--17---
						--18----	--18----	--18---
						--19----	--19----	--19---
						--20----	--20----	--20---

Coach—Johnny Sorrell   Trainer—Less Tooke

Here is the Capitals' lineup from a game against the St. Louis Flyers. Several players from the Caps' lineup went on to the NHL. The Flyers were one of the Capitals' main rivals.

23

Rollie "Rosy" Rossignol, Les Douglas, and Jud McAtee in the 1945–46 season. Rossignol only played 48 games in Indy, but Douglas and McAtee became two of the most decorated players in team history. Douglas held the team records for most goals (5) and assists (5) in a game and, with 268 points, was the team's third-leading career scorer. He was also the all-time assists leader with 167. McAtee totaled 123 points in 193 games with the Caps, from 1940 to 1943 and in 1945–46. (Courtesy of the Indiana Historical Society/Bass Photo collection #26556F-1.)

Goaltender Tom Wilson began an incredible streak 24 seconds into the third period against the Hershey Bears January 5, 1946. For the next 217 minutes and 34 seconds, nobody would be able to push a puck past Wilson. He shut out the St. Louis Flyers, Pittsburgh Hornets, and Providence Reds in back-to-back games—the latter two being the first for new coach Earl Seibert. Wilson's streak ended late in the first period of a January 12 game in St. Louis. (Courtesy of the Indiana Historical Society/Bass Photo collection #65456F-14.)

INDIANAPOLIS CAPITALS—AMERICAN HOCKEY LEAGUE—1946-1947

The 1946–47 Indianapolis Capitals became the best team in hockey history to miss the postseason, posting a 33-18-13 record. A nearly-identical mark the year before won the division. Team members, from left to right, are pictured as follows: (front row) Gerry Couture, Thain Simon, trainer/goaltender Lefty Wilson, coach Tommy Ivan, Ralph "Red" Almas, Al Dewsbury, and Bob Weist; (middle row) Tony Licari, Nels Podolsky, Cliff Simpson, Tony Bukovich, Sam Kennedy, and Hugh Millar; (back row) Ed Nicholson, Steve Wochy, Enio Scilisizzi, Don Simmons, Bruce Burdette, Rod Morrison, and George Blake. The Capitals' secondary logo, a block "I" inside a "C", is visible on the sleeves of Wilson, Dewsbury, and Nicholson's sweaters.

The 1947–48 Capitals put together a big offensive year but missed the postseason. Team members, from left to right, are pictured as follows: (front row) Nels Podolsky, Enio Scilisizzi, goaltender Ralph "Red" Almas, Tony Licari, and Calum McKay; (middle row) trainer Ross "Lefty" Wilson, Lee Fogolin, Thain Simon, Barry Sullivan, Gerry Couture, Cliff Simpson, Lloyd Doran, and coach Johnny Mowers; (back row) Hugh Millar, Ed Bruneteau, Pat Lundy, Ed Nicholson, and Dan Summers. Cliff Simpson set a team record with 110 points. In one late six-game stretch, he had 12 goals and 10 assists. Note the new uniforms, which simply had the letter "C" on each sleeve.

Ott Heller, Cliff Simpson, Ed Nicholson and Don Morrison pictured during the 1948–49 season. Heller became the Capitals' player-coach that season, beginning a four-year stint with the club in which the team would post a 134-110-32 mark, making him the winningest coach in Indianapolis professional hockey history. Simpson was coming off an incredible year in which he had 48 goals, 62 assists, and 110 points. He and Providence's Carl Liscombe (118 points) became the AHL's first 100-point scorers that year. Simpson would leave the Caps as the team's all-time leader in points (281) and goals (136). Nicholson was a steady defenseman who played 187 games with the team. (Courtesy of the Indiana Historical Society/Bass Photo collection. Photo unnumbered.)

Terry Sawchuk is flanked by Fred Glover (left) and Frank Melong. The first two professional seasons in Sawchuk's long Hall of Fame career were spent playing for the Indianapolis Capitals. He led the Caps to an eight-game sweep of the 1950 Calder Cup playoffs, posting a 3.07 goals against average along the way. Glover went on to become the AHL's career scoring leader. He totaled 229 points with the Caps from 1948 to 1952, the team's final four seasons. (Courtesy of the Indiana Historical Society/Bass Photo collection No. 273000F-1.)

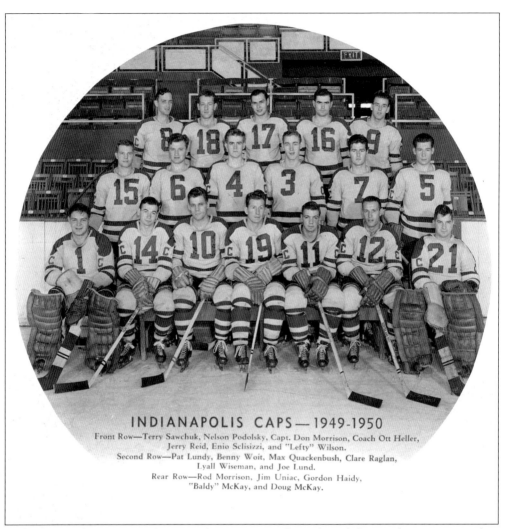

INDIANAPOLIS CAPS — 1949-1950

Front Row—Terry Sawchuk, Nelson Podolsky, Capt. Don Morrison, Coach Ott Heller,
Jerry Reid, Enio Sclisizzi, and "Lefty" Wilson.
Second Row—Pat Lundy, Benny Woit, Max Quackenbush, Clare Raglan,
Lyall Wiseman, and Joe Lund.
Rear Row—Rod Morrison, Jim Uniac, Gordon Haidy,
"Baldy" McKay, and Doug McKay.

The 1949–50 Calder Cup championship team members, from left to right, are pictured as follows: (front row) Terry Sawchuk, Nelson Podolsky, Don Morrison, coach Ott Heller, Jerry Reid, Enio Scilisizzi, and trainer/backup goaltender Ross "Lefty" Wilson; (middle row) Pat Lundy, Benny Woit, Max Quackenbush, Clare "Rags" Raglan, Lyall Wiseman, and Joe Lund; (back row) Rod Morrison, Jim Uniac, Gordon Haidy, Lloyd "Baldy" McKay, and Doug McKay. The Caps finished second in the AHL's West Division, but swept Providence, St. Louis, and Cleveland in the playoffs to win the Cup. (Courtesy of the Indiana Historical Society/Bass Photo collection #72546F-29.)

Defenseman Clare Raglan poses for a traditional individual photograph of the era. Raglan played two years with the Caps. (Courtesy of the Indiana State Fairgrounds.)

Enio Scilisizzi, Don Morrison, and Rod Morrison pose. The trio formed the heart and soul of the Capitals' attack in the franchise's later years. All three joined the Caps for long stints after World War II. Scilisizzi was a popular player who tallied 280 points from 1946 to 1952. Don Morrison was the team's captain and played with the Caps from 1947 to 1950. His brother Rod played more games in a Capital uniform than anyone else (319, five more than Scilisizzi), and totaled 218 points in a career that began in Indy in 1943–44 and continued in the Circle City from 1946 to 1951. (Courtesy of the Indiana Historical Society/Bass Photo collection. Photo unnumbered.)

This program is from the Capitals' final season in Indianapolis, the 1951–52 campaign. The increasing influence of television and other diversions caused the Caps' crowds to dwindle. With a number of new faces, it was a young team that struggled on the ice—although the lineup (below) featured future Hall of Famer, goaltender Glenn Hall, who is credited with inventing the "butterfly" style of goaltending that would become popular 40 years later. The Caps went 22-40-6 that season, and saw attendance numbers that once averaged close to 8,000 dwindle into the 4,000 range. Toward the end of the year, general manager Dick Miller took over the team and talked of moving it into a Midwestern-based league. But the Caps never played another game.

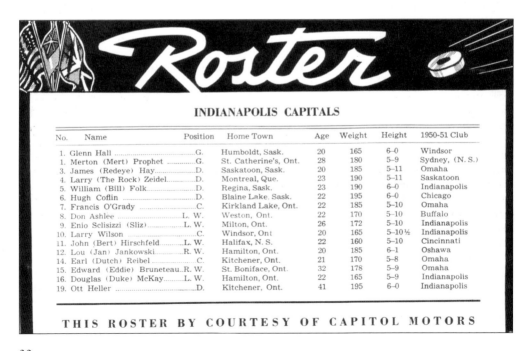

Roster

INDIANAPOLIS CAPITALS

No.	Name	Position	Home Town	Age	Weight	Height	1950-51 Club
1.	Glenn Hall	G.	Humboldt, Sask.	20	165	6–0	Windsor
1.	Merton (Mert) Prophet	G.	St. Catherine's, Ont.	28	180	5–9	Sydney, (N. S.)
3.	James (Redeye) Hay	D.	Saskatoon, Sask.	20	185	5–11	Omaha
4.	Larry (The Rock) Zeidel	D.	Montreal, Que.	23	190	5–11	Saskatoon
5.	William (Bill) Folk	D.	Regina, Sask.	23	190	6–0	Indianapolis
6.	Hugh Coflin	D.	Blaine Lake, Sask.	22	195	6–0	Chicago
7.	Francis O'Grady	C.	Kirkland Lake, Ont.	22	185	5–10	Omaha
8.	Don Ashlee	L. W.	Weston, Ont.	22	170	5–10	Buffalo
9.	Enio Sclisizzi (Sliz)	L. W.	Milton, Ont.	26	172	5–10	Indianapolis
10.	Larry Wilson	C.	Windsor, Ont.	20	165	5–10½	Indianapolis
11.	John (Bert) Hirschfeld	L. W.	Halifax, N. S.	22	160	5–10	Cincinnati
12.	Lou (Jan) Jankowski	R. W.	Hamilton, Ont.	20	185	6–1	Oshawa
14.	Earl (Dutch) Reibel	C.	Kitchener, Ont.	21	170	5–8	Omaha
15.	Edward (Eddie) Bruneteau	R. W.	St. Boniface, Ont.	32	178	5–9	Omaha
16.	Douglas (Duke) McKay	L. W.	Hamilton, Ont.	22	165	5–9	Indianapolis
19.	Ott Heller	D.	Kitchener, Ont.	41	195	6–0	Indianapolis

THREE

Transitions

CHIEFS 1955–1962, CAPITALS 1963

In 1952, Capitals general manager Dick Miller spoke of a new Great Lakes hockey league—with the AHL franchises in Indianapolis and Cincinnati mentioned as possible entries, as well as nearby markets in Fort Wayne, Louisville, Toledo, and Grand Rapids. Miller's dream came three years too late for the fledgling Capitals, who became a victim of timing in 1952 and could no longer compete in the high-dollar AHL.

With the rise of television, attendance and revenue went down. Throw in the fact that train travel—the preferred mode of conveyance of AHL teams in the 1940s—was beginning to decline, and the league suddenly became cost-prohibitive. Indianapolis and Cincinnati were the first to go, in 1952, and St. Louis failed a year later.

Nevertheless, the league Miller dreamed of was forming in the body of a pre-existing league—the International Hockey League, which was founded in Detroit in 1946 and slowly grew throughout the Midwest in the early 1950s. After the Capitals' demise in 1952 Indianapolis became a perfect market for the expanding IHL—which encompassed all of the markets Miller had spoken of three years earlier.

Mel Ross managed an 8,000-seat ice rink that had been sitting empty for three years in a certain large midwestern city. In an era when low costs were vital due to increased competition that brought down attendance—from television and drive-in theaters—the IHL offered many advantages. All of the league's franchises were based in Ohio, Michigan, and Indiana, allowing for bus travel. Also, the circuit's semi-pro status meant player costs wouldn't be high. It was the perfect marriage—a low-cost league with an available building in a market that had shown a passion for hockey over the previous decade.

Against that backdrop, Ross was given a franchise, which he named the Chiefs, and Indianapolis had a new minor league team. One of Ross' first moves was to establish a tie to the old days, naming former Capitals mentor John Sorrell coach. Sorrell was one of several familiar faces in the new IHL club—ex-Capitals Nels Podolsky (Troy), Doug McCaig (Fort Wayne), and Rollie McLenahan (Cincinnati) were also IHL coaches. After 13 years of affiliation with the Detroit Red Wings, the new franchise would operate as an independent.

After a three-week training camp, Sorrell's charges donned their red and white uniforms and skated out onto the Coliseum ice for the first time October 16. A crowd of 3,000 turned out for the Sunday matinee—Sunday was still hockey day in Indianapolis.

Bob Lalonde donned the goaltender pads and the oversized No. 1 jersey to play goal. Starting in front of him were Ed St. Louis and Bernie Hill on defense. Maurice Lamirande centered, with Roger Hayfield and Billy Kawulia up front against the Grand Rapids Hornets. Lalonde stopped a late breakaway and the Chiefs won their opener 3-2. The Chiefs won their next game against the Fort Wayne Komets, but the wins soon came few and far between: the team lost 22 of their next 23 games—several by lopsided scores. The worst was a 15-3 drubbing in Fort Wayne. During one game, the Coliseum organist began playing a song with the lyrics "Give me some men who are stout-hearted men, who will fight for the rights they adore."

Sorrell left for Canada to find players. After the Chiefs fell to 5-29-0, Leo Lamoureux, one of the players Sorrell found on his trip, replaced him as coach. The team improved slightly but finished the season 11-48-1, a record for futile efforts in the IHL that would last until the 1970s.

The first season was a learning experience for everyone. The 1956-57 year would bring something completely different. Lamoureux replaced most of the roster, with most of the buzz centering around the "B" line, Pierre Brillant, Marc Boileau, and Bob Bowness. These players combined to form one of the IHL's top lines over the next two seasons. The trio combined for 94 goals in 1956–57 and 95 the next season.

"Pierre should've been in the NHL. He was small. He never really got a chance. He didn't like to go into the corners too much, but Bob Bowness would go into the corners. Marc Boileau was a great play maker and Pierre could thread the eye of a needle. He loved offense. You didn't ever look for him to come to the other side of the blue line, but he loved offense," said Cliff Hicks, the team's goaltender from 1956 to 1959.

Hicks was another player Lamoureux brought in. A former New York Rangers prospect, Hicks was discovered when he played against Lamoureux's team in eastern Canada. Lamoureux remembered the goaltender, and called and asked him to come to Indianapolis.

"Leo was a very, very good tactician. He was strict, but he was a player's coach. He got along with the players," Hicks said. "He was fundamentally sound. He grew up in the Montreal organization, which was a fundamentally sound club. Leo knew hockey. If he had a weakness, it was you could get under his skin. Other teams would know that and try."

The "B" line was as good as advertised and Hicks was a wall in goal—he gave up seven goals in a seven-game winning streak and had two shutouts in 1956–57. The Chiefs remained in postseason contention all year and clinched second place despite finishing 26-29-5. Brillant won the league scoring title with 78 points and was named the league's MVP. Linemates Bowness and Boileau also scored 20 goals apiece.

The Chiefs matched up with the Toledo Mercurys in their first-ever playoff series, and won in five games; George Hayes scored a goal 1:49 into the third period of the deciding fifth game and Hicks made it stand up for a 3-2 game and series victory. The Cincinnati Mohawks—the league's only team to finish with a winning record (50-9-1)—flexed their muscle in the Turner Cup Finals, dispatching the Chiefs 4-1, 7-1, and 5-0 to win their fifth straight IHL championship. Ross hoped for greener pastures after the difficult maiden voyage, but attendance still averaged 2,400. However, he said the team broke even after first year losses of $50,000.

The best was yet to come. The team's core was back for the 1957–58 season. The league aimed for mighty Cincinnati, which had never lost a championship since joining the league. While Toledo's general manager claimed the Mohawks were violating the league's salary cap and should be expelled from the IHL, Lamoureux said, "Why not just go out and get better talent than Cincinnati?" In spite of a last-place standing, Lamoureux tried to be the team to unseat the Mohawks.

The Chiefs finished fourth, going 28-30-6, but they were the only team in the league to post a winning record against Cincinnati. Brillant was an All-Star for the second straight year, this time scoring 71 points. But Bowness took team scoring honors with 26 goals and 61 assists. To get to Cincinnati, the Chiefs needed to get past the Fort Wayne Komets. The Chiefs treaded up an ice-covered State Road 37 to open the series, and split the first two games. Back home, Brillant scored a hat trick in an 8-2 Game 3 victory, and Hicks posted a 3-0 shutout in Game 4 to send the Chiefs to the Turner Cup Finals for the second straight year. But the Cincinnati Mohawks' reign had ended. The Louisville Rebels—a first-year team that had become a bitter rival of the Chiefs—upset Cincinnati and advanced to the finals.

Things didn't look good for the Chiefs. Hicks broke his thumb early in the series, the last five games had to be played in Louisville, and the Rebels had a 3-2 series lead with a chance to win it all in overtime of Game 6. But Chief Alex Viskelis took a pass across the goalmouth and scored a power-play goal eight minutes into the extra session to extend the Chiefs' season one more game. They made it count. Myron Stankiewicz put the Chiefs up 2-0 in the deciding seventh game with a goal and an assist. Louisville scored early in the second, but Brillant drew Louisville goaltender Lou Crowdis out of his net and fed Boileau for a goal that made it 3-1. Louisville staged an all-out assault on Hicks' net. The Rebels scored once but couldn't finish the game off. The Chiefs were Turner Cup champions!

"We had a good-skating hockey club. As long as you have good skating and goaltending, you'll go very far. When you add to that Boileau and Brillant up front who can make plays and score goals, we had a little offense to go with it. We had primarily good defense with a little bit of offense," Hicks said. "Starting before the playoffs [in 1958], we had become a good unit. Everybody got along. There was no dissension. . . . Nobody was going to beat us once we got into the playoffs."

Boileau and Brillant were named to the IHL's First All-Star team. Hicks and coach Lamoureux were second-teamers. For the second straight year, Brillant was given the James Gatschene Trophy for the IHL's Most Outstanding Player.

The turner Cup victory was the highlight of the Chiefs' seven-year run in Indianapolis. The next year, former Louisville coach Max Silverman bought a piece of the team, made himself coach, and overhauled the team. Five players returned—including Hicks, Viskelis, and Brillant—but many key players left, including Bowness and Boileau. Brillant had to take on more of the scoring load and he put in his highest-scoring season as a Chief—totaling 57 goals and 98 points. The team finished 26-30-4, but Fort Wayne beat the Chiefs 4-1 in the opening round of the playoffs.

That season's highlight came January 7, 1959. WTTV's cameras entered the Coliseum and brought hockey into Hoosier living rooms. The game was joined in progress so that television viewership would not take away from ticket sales. Those who watched saw the Chiefs beat the Toledo Mercurys 7-1, with newcomer Rene St. Hiliare scoring a hat trick.

The Chiefs had another new coach in 1959–60, Marcel Clements, and a handful of new opponents—teams in Omaha, Denver, St. Paul, and Milwaukee. They also had a new home rink, playing a handful of games in Cincinnati. But the season never got off the ground—the Chiefs lost their first nine games, including a stretch in which they lost 9-3, 12-3, and 14-2 in back-to-back games. Brillant missed the first two games, holding out for additional compensation, although he scored 50 goals for the second straight year. A young defense hung Hicks—the backstop of three playoff teams—out to dry. He left the team after a 2-12-0 start. The team rebounded to go 22-14-3 in the middle of the season but lost 13 of its last 14 games to finish 25-40-3.

The 1960–61 season wasn't marked as much for its 20-46-4 record, but because of two major events that changed the face of the team. The most notable was the untimely mid-season death of coach Leo Lamoureux. He returned to Indianapolis after a two-year hiatus to coach the Chiefs. In his two-and-a-half years with the team, he led them to the Turner Cup Finals in 1957 and the championship in 1958. On the team's season-opening road trip, Lamoureux took ill and left the team. He died on January 10.

Just days before Lamoureux's death, the last vestiges of the Turner Cup championship team was traded away, as Brillant—the Chiefs' most recognizable name and scoring leader—was traded to the Omaha Knights. He had tallied 204 goals, 161 assists and 365 points in 278 games and won the IHL's MVP trophy twice.

The team didn't fare any better in 1961-62, going 19-49-0. Coach Alex Shibicky left at the end of the season to look for players for the next fall. But there wouldn't be a next fall; Ross couldn't take the financial burden anymore and shut down the team.

This time, Indianapolis was without hockey for one full year. Then, in the fall of 1963, an old friend—the Detroit Red Wings—brought hockey back to Indianapolis.

The new team was christened the Capitols—not to be confused with the Capitals of a decade before—and they were one of five teams in the new Central Professional Hockey League. Like its predecessors, this team would be filled with Red Wing prospects. Tony Leswick was named coach. The Capitols' run was short—nine games. Their only win was a forfeit—a St. Louis team owned by former Capitals owner Arthur Wirtz feared its equipment would be seized due to litigation (against Wirtz). So, the Braves never showed up, the puck dropped and the Indianapolis Capitols garnered their only win. The promise of a team to match those that played in the AHL over a decade ago went unfulfilled. While the Capitols were in the middle of a long road trip, an explosion at the Coliseum closed the building. The building was shuttered for renovation, and the team finished their road trip and went straight to Cincinnati, where they played the balance of the season.

The 1956–57 Chiefs team finished second in the league and advanced to the Turner Cup Finals after several key off-season acquisitions. Team members, from left to right, are as follows: (front row) George Hayes, Pierre Brillant, Jack Douglas, Cliff Hicks, Bob Bowness, Gerry Lamoureux, and Ed Calhoun; (back row) coach Leo Lamoureux, Lloyd McKey, Don Busch, Doug Kilburn, Frank Kuzma, Pete Wywrot, Marc Boileau, Myron Stankiewicz, trainer Ken Storey, and owner Mel Ross. (Thelma Bowness collection, courtesy of Al Josey.)

34

Pictured are the 1957–58 Turner Cup champions. The Chiefs rallied to win the last two games and clinched the title in seven games against Louisville. Team members, from left to right, are: (front row) Norm Willey, Myron Stankiewicz, Cliff Hicks, coach Leo Lamoureux, Marc Boileau, owner Mel Ross, Ron Morgan, Sam Gregory, and trainer Ken Storey; (back row) Alex Viskelis, Germain "Red" Leger, Frank Kuzma, Pierre Brillant, Don Busch, Bill Short, and Lloyd McKey. Not pictured is Bob Bowness. (Thelma Bowness collection, courtesy of Al Josey.)

There was plenty of action between the Caps and the Omaha Knights. Bob Cox (8) and Wayne Muloin battle an Omaha player for the puck in the corner at the Coliseum in 1963. The Caps played only five games at the Coliseum before a deadly propane explosion October 31, 1963, caused the arena to be closed. On November 6, with the team midway through a four-game road trip, it was announced the Capitols would finish the season as the Cincinnati Wings. (Courtesy of the Paul O'Neill collection.)

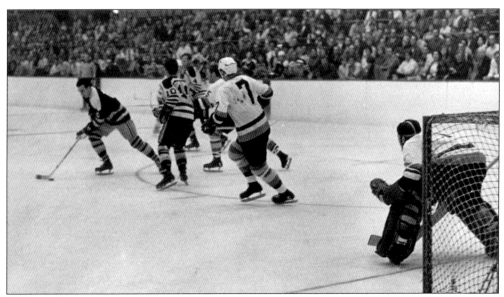

More action is seen here during a game at the Coliseum, *circa* 1969. While Indianapolis did not have a professional hockey team from the demise of the Capitals until 1974, a handful of games were played on the premises. (Courtesy of the Indiana State Fairgrounds.)

FOUR

The Big Leagues

RACERS 1974–1978

In the 1970s, Indianapolis was beginning to shed its image as a "Naptown"—the sleepy city in between Chicago, Cincinnati, Detroit, and St. Louis. Its only big-time diversion was the Indianapolis 500 and an upstart American Basketball Association franchise called the Indiana Pacers.

At the same time, major-league sports were exploding—with rapid expansion and rival leagues in nearly every major professional sport. The National Football League merged with the competing American Football League and grew from 12 teams to 26—and a new competitor sprung up, the World Football League. Major League Baseball grew from 16 teams to 24. The National Basketball Association found competition in the upstart ABA—which included the wildly successful Indiana Pacers, winners of three league titles.

The Pacers had filled the Fairgrounds Coliseum during hockey's absence. They were one of the ABA's charter franchises in 1967 and immediately won the hearts of an adoring city hungry for big-time sports.

But there was room for more. Hockey was growing rapidly—the National Hockey League doubled in size from six teams in 1967 to 12 the next year, and had plans to grow to 16 by the mid-1970s. But that was no enough. Gary Davidson and Bill Hunter—the brains behind the ABA and WFL—wanted to give the NHL a rival, too.

In that environment, the World Hockey Association came into existence. Indianapolis had been without hockey since the Coliseum explosion forced the Capitols to move to Cincinnati in 1963. But with pro leagues exploding, it was a big-league city ripe for expansion into the WHA, especially when the city began building Market Square Arena, a multipurpose building on the east side of downtown that would host the Pacers, major concerts, events, and hopefully a new professional hockey team. Scheduled to open in 1974, the WHA granted Paul Deneau and Indianapolis a franchise for the league's third season.

The team was named the Indianapolis Racers, paying homage to the famous racetrack, and the Indianapolis 500 run annually a few miles away. Red, white, and blue were chosen as the team's colors and Gerry Moore was named the new team's first coach.

The Racers filled their roster via an expansion draft. They chose the Edmonton Oilers' Brian

McKenzie with their first pick. They also drafted Bob Whitlock and Bob Sicinski, two players who would make a big impact in years to come. Andy Brown—one of the last remaining goaltenders to play without a mask—was lured away from the NHL's Pittsburgh Penguins to play in net, and the Racers had a team.

The Racers played their first game October 17, 1974, against the Michigan Stags, a game they lost 4-2. The first-year record reflected the Racers' expansion status. They played 78 games and won only 18. They lost their first five games, before beating the Quebec Nordiques 5-3 on October 27. They went 1-19 in one 20-game stretch early in the season and lost their last 10 games.

The roster was in flux, as Moore and general manager Jim Browitt tried to find players to stop the slide; the Racers picked up 12 players from other WHA teams during the year, including future mainstays Brian McDonald and Ken Block. But the expansion draft picks led the team in scoring. Whitlock totaled 31 goals and 57 points, while Sicinski had 19 goals and 53 points.

After the Racers struggled out of the gate again in 1975-76 and lost four of their first five games, Moore was fired. Jacques Demers, the team's player personnel director, was introduced as the new head coach after the fourth loss. Play-by-play announcer Bob Lamey made the change public after the game, saying Demers was surprised by his new role and hadn't even had time to inform his wife of the new duties.

With Demers at the helm, a 31-year-old who had never coached a professional team, the Racer's fortunes changed. A 6-2 victory at Toronto in mid-November set the stage for an 8-2-0 stretch that got the Racers to the .500 mark for the first time in team history. The East division turned out to be the weakest of the WHA's three divisions that season, and a team that caught fire could make a run for the title. Four mid-season pickups proved key, as the Racers added Rene LeClerc and Michel Parizeau from Quebec, Hugh Harris from Calgary and Darryl Maggs from Denver. Defenseman Pat Stapleton came over to anchor the blueline. By late February though, the Racers were 23-35-2 and trailed second-place Cleveland and Cincinnati by seven points; their playoff hopes appeared dead. But the Minnesota Fighting Saints couldn't meet payroll and folded February 28. Not only did this give the Racers one less team to beat in the playoff chase, it also delivered future Hall of Famer Dave Keon to Indianapolis.

A big change in momentum took hold of the team the same day the Saints folded. The Racers trailed 4-2 after two periods in New England, but Kim Clackson buried Nick Fotiu in a legendary fight that turned the match around, and LeClerc scored with 1:20 left to tie the game at 4-4. The tie gave the Racers life. The Racers trailed Cincinnati by double-digits in the standings, but beat the Stingers three times over the next week. A 4-1 deficit in Phoenix became a 6-4 win. They moved into second place, beating Cleveland 3-2, and then knocked off New England 3-1 March 28—finishing a 7-0-3 stretch that vaulted them from last place to first. They finished off the run with a 3-1 victory over Toronto four nights later. The Racers clinched the division title with a 35-39-6 record on the last day of the season when San Diego beat Cleveland.

"Even looking back, I don't know how that happened," Lamey said. "Jacques Demers was a good players' coach and he was good with the fans. The players and the fans in the city built an incredible camaraderie. You can't legislate that. It just has to happen. Toward the middle of the year, I remember a game where we just had to get some points. We had a bunch of injuries and started Leif Holmquist in goal and came out with a 4-4 tie. We kind of started building on that. We won a lot of games we weren't supposed to win."

Goaltender Michel Dion led the league with a 2.74 goals against average. Nick Harbaruk, Reggie Thomas, and mid-season acquisition Blair McDonald broke the 20-goal mark.

The Racers met the New England Whalers in the playoffs and promptly got locked into a tight best-of-7 series. They lost three of the first four games, but Dion blanked the Whalers 4-0 in Game 5, and the Racers bounced back to win Game 6 5-3 in Hartford. Back at MSA, with 16,040 fans cheering the team on, New England spoiled the party with a 6-0 victory to take the series in seven games. Even so,10,000 remaining fans gave the Racers a noisy standing ovation when the game ended, showing just how much affection can build up between fans and a team.

"The people in the seats were fans," Lamey said. "It created a love affair between the players and the people who bought tickets. It transcended all boundaries. There was no reason for people to show up at certain points during the season. There was no reason for them getting into the team the way they did. I remember going out to my car after Game 7, and someone asked me, 'When does next season start?' It wasn't a loss. There was so much positive happening. That seventh game didn't mean much."

The Racers had momentum going into the next season—a loyal fan base, Demers back for his second season as coach, and a core of returning players, including Dion, Stapleton, Block, Sicinski, Parizeau, Harris, Maggs, and LeClerc. They also added Gene Peacosh at midseason, which would be big later on. They were bothered by injuries most of the year, but won six of their last 11 games to roll into the playoffs with a 36-37-8 mark. Blair MacDonald was the leading goal scorer with 34, while Maggs' 55 assists led to a team-high 71 points.

The Racers and the Cincinnati Stingers were evenly matched in the first round with the Stingers slight favorites. But it was one of those series where everything changed in the opening game. Game 1, in Riverfront Coliseum, the Stingers' home, drew 12,429 fans. Through regulation, the teams played to a 3-3 draw, with Mark Lomenda scoring twice for the Racers. That's where the drama began. Nobody scored in the first overtime. A second yielded no goals. Players were beginning to tire. So were the fans—the clock was closing in on 1 a.m. They had long ago passed the WHA longest-game record.

"The thing you had to fight was getting lazy mentally," Peacosh said in a Racers program story. "You'd look at the puck and think you wouldn't take the extra step to get it and let somebody else pick it up. You had to make yourself go at it."

Peacosh became the hero. Midway through the third overtime, Lomenda carried the puck up the middle. He fired a shot wide, but the puck bounced off the end boards straight to Peacosh in the right circle. Goaltender Norm LaPointe didn't have time to react. Peacosh fired and scored. He found himself under a mound of teammates after 108 minutes and 40 seconds—at 1:16 in the morning. The Racers won the game 4-3. The series was virtually over at that point.

"I remember the bus ride back from Cincinnati that night," Lamey said. "You knew who was going to win the series from that point on. They were pretty good. We were supposed to be out in four or five games."

The Racers beat the Stingers 7-2 and 5-3 in the next two games before finishing the series with a 3-1 victory at Market Square Arena. Eventual Avco Cup champion Quebec would eliminate the Racers in five games in the Eastern Division final, but the Racers had hit their mountaintop in their brief tenure.

The end of their run was near. Financial troubles had bubbled under the surface through the team's first three years. The team nearly folded in 1977, but Canadian Nelson Skalbania purchased the team. Virtually everything changed. Demers went to greener pastures in Cincinnati, as did several players—including Stapleton and Dion. Ken Block and Michel Parizeau were among the few holdovers who remained and spent the entire season in Indianapolis. The team struggled. Newcomer Claude St. Sauveur scored 36 goals and 75 points, setting team records. But the team gave up four goals per game, with Gary Inness and three others sharing net duties. With two different coaches, the Racers lost 51 games and finished in last place.

The team made one big move before it folded, signing 17-year-old phenom Wayne Gretzky (one reason for optimism in the Racers camp in the fall of 1978). Stapleton returned to coach the squad but he didn't want to play Gretzky too much too early. The rookie made an impression in his pro debut, scoring two goals and adding an assist in an exhibition game. Goaltender Gary Smith said Gretzky was the best passer in hockey. Stapleton said he moved the puck well to both sides, but added "he's not a great goal scorer." He wasn't a household name yet— the *Indianapolis Star's* headline the next day misspelled his name "Gretsky."

He was impressive, although scoreless, in his regular-season debut, a 6-3 loss to Winnipeg. He scored his first two professional goals October 20 against the Edmonton Oilers—the team for which he would win four Stanley Cup titles in the NHL. The points came 37 seconds apart midway through the second period. Radio announcer Mike Fornes called the initial one "the first of many goals that will be scored by Wayne Gretzky."

But the financial troubles never went away. The team was drawing 5,000 fans per game and was rumored due to fold at the end of October. Gretzky scored three goals and had three assists in the Racers' first eight games, but the team was 2-5-1. Facing financial difficulty, Skalbania sold the young star—along with goaltender Ed Mio and wing Peter Driscoll—to the Edmonton Oilers for a sum reported to be $850,000. Several front-office members were also let go. Shortly thereafter, Rich Leduc and Kevin Morrison were dealt to Quebec for virtually nothing—draft choices that were never used. The Racers did sign junior Mark Messier out of the deal, who played five games in Indianapolis to begin his Hall of Fame career.

But without their star players, the Racers fell into last place at 5-18-2. The end was near by mid-December. They played their final game in front of 4,623 fans, with Angie Morretto scoring the final goal with 1:45 left in a 7-4 loss to the New England Whalers December 12. Three days later, with a Soviet All-Star team scheduled to visit that night, Skalbania folded the team: he was unable to come up with enough money to keep the team afloat—players were owed two paychecks. Skalbania claimed he lost $1.2 million during his tenure. The WHA closed shop, and four teams—Edmonton, New England, Winnipeg, and Quebec—merged into the National Hockey League the next year.

The end came bitterly for the Racers, just two seasons removed from their run as toast of the town. This sole flirtation with big-time hockey in Indianapolis ended with a thud. But memories of the brief love affair remain. Many of the players settled in Indiana. In 1999, the Indianapolis Ice paid homage, wearing replica uniforms. It took nearly an hour to exhaust the line of fans who turned out to meet Peter Driscoll, Michel Dion, and several other ex-players. Like the WHA, the Racers have become a memory. Of all the years hockey has been played in Indianapolis, none have been remembered more fondly than the Racers' colorful four and a half winters of big-league hockey.

The Racers began playing during the 1974–75 season, introducing Indianapolis to big-league hockey and ending an 11-year hiatus without hockey that had lasted since 1963. The inaugural Racers, from left to right, were: (front row) Andy Brown, Jim Johnson, Bob Woytowich, coach Gerry Moore, Bob Sicinski, president/general manager James W. Browitt, Ken Block, Bob Ash, and Ed Dyck; (back row) assistant trainer Fraser Gleason, Bob Whitlock, Ken Desjardine, Dick Proceviat, Kerry Bond, John Sheridan, Ron Buchanan, Joe Hardy, Bob Fitchner, Nick Harbaruk, Bill Horton, Jim Wiste, Brian McDonald, and trainer Bill Carroll. (Courtesy of the Spade collection.)

Kim Clackson became a folk hero in Indianapolis for his ability to use his fists. During the "frontier days" of hockey in the late 1970s, Clackson was the Racers' policeman. He totaled 519 penalty minutes in a two-season stint with the club. A win in a fight against New England's Nick Fotiu in March 1976 turned around a game the Racers eventually tied. The result sparked a streak that led to the Racers winning the division title.

Andy Brown was the last professional hockey goaltender to play without a mask. He backstopped the Racers in each of the team's first three seasons, winning 23 games and posting a 3.94 goals against average. (Courtesy of Judy Stuart/Racers Booster Club.)

Magazine

Brian McDonald

Brian McDonald was dubbed "Big Mac" during his years with the Racers. Acquired midway through the team's first season, the right wing was a stalwart for the team over the next two years. He totaled 45 goals and 45 assists in those three seasons. Here, he is pictured on the cover of the February 18, 1975, program for a game between the Racers and the Vancouver Blazers. (Courtesy of the Indianapolis Racers.)

PHOTOGRAPHY BY ES
PRINTED BY ADVERTISERS WEB PRESS / PHOENIX

The Racers began the season in the basement, but eventually shot up to first place in the WHA's East Division in 1975–76, winning the title despite posting a 35-39-6 record. The Racers then fought New England to a tight seven-game series before falling in the final game in front of a sellout crowd at Market Square Arena. Team members, from left to right, are: (front row) Andy Brown, Bob Sicinski, Murray Heatley, Dick Proceviat, Jacques Demers, coach Gerry Moore, Bob Woytowich, general manager Jim Browitt, chairman Paul Deneau, Ron Buchanan, Pat Stapleton, Ken Block, and Leif Holmquist; (back row) trainer Fraser Gleason, Kim Clackson, Jim Wiste, Al Karlander, Ted Scharf, Reggie Thomas, John Sheridan, Nick Harbaruk, Bob Fitchner, Randy Wyrozub, Brian Coates, Michael Dubois, Bob Whitlock, and two unidentified staff. This photo was taken early in the season. As the season progressed, the Racers added nine key players and replaced Moore with Demers as coach. (Courtesy of the Spade collection.)

Leif Holmquist skates before a game against the Quebec Nordiques in 1975–76 in Le Colise.

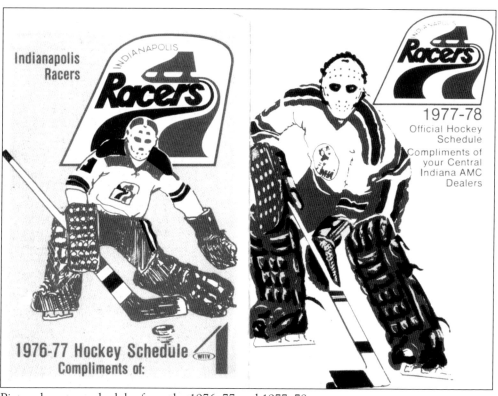

Pictured are two schedules from the 1976–77 and 1977–78 seasons.

Gary Inness became one of the Racers' goaltenders in 1977–78. His red-and-blue mask became memorialized in the Hockey Hall of Fame in Toronto. (Courtesy of Judy Stuart/ Racers Booster Club.)

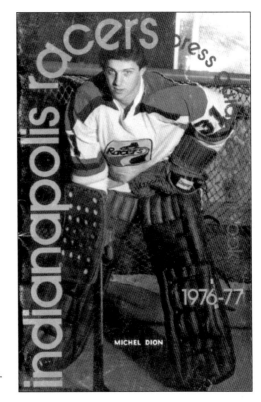

Michel Dion joined the team during its first season and became its primary backstop by 1975–76. He posted a team record 2.74 goals against average that season, leading the team to the division championship. The next year, he graced the cover of the team's media guide. (Courtesy of the Indianapolis Racers.)

The Racers made a number of changes going into the 1977–78 season. Among them: a new coach; a new owner, Nelson Skalbania; and a virtually new roster. The members of the team, from left to right, are pictured as follows: (front row) Ed Mio, Barry Wilkins, Rusty Patenaude, vice president Don LaRose, Gary Inness, player-coach Bill Goldsworthy, captain Ken Block, Rosaire Paiment, and Jim Park; (second row) Renald LeClerc, Bill Prentice, Peter Driscoll, Charles Constantin, Dave Inkpen, Rich Leduc, Glen Irwin, Blaine Stoughton, and Kevin Morrison; (back row) trainer Bill Carroll, Dave Fortier, Claude Larose, Don Burgess, John French, Michel Parizeau, Kevin Devine, Giles Marotte, Claude St. Sauveur, and assistant trainer John Carey. The Racers went 24-51-5 that year, but saw St. Sauveur set a club record with 78 points. (Courtesy of the Spade collection.)

Ken Block and Rene LeClerc line up for a faceoff against the Quebec Nordiques. Block became the face of the Racers during his tenure. He was the only player to be on the team in all five of its seasons. He played 267 games. He scored just seven goals but was fifth all-time in team history with 80 assists. LeClerc totaled 133 points in four seasons with the Racers.

Here is another view of Block, the Racers' captain. (Courtesy of Judy Stuart/ Racers Booster Club.)

The most decorated Racer—and hockey player—of all time, Wayne Gretzky began his storied career with the Racers when he signed a personal services contract with team owner Nelson Skalbania in 1978. Just 17 years old, Gretzky scored his first three professional goals as a member of the Racers—the first two October 20, 1978, against the Edmonton Oilers, a team he would later lead to four Stanley Cup championships. Gretzky's presence produced a stir in Indianapolis—department store L.S. Ayres had a "Great Gretzky Fan Club." But the buzz wasn't yet quite enough. After an exhibition game, a local newspaper misspelled his name in a headline and Gretztky's presence didn't bring in the necessary numbers at the box office. After eight games as a Racer, Skalbania dealt Gretzky to the Oilers, along with Peter Driscoll and Ed Mio, for an infusion of cash and some draft picks that everyone knew would never be used. Gretzky totaled three goals and three assists in eight games in Indianapolis. The Racers went 2-5-1 in that span and folded 17 games after his sale to Edmonton. Gretztky went on to hold every major NHL scoring record. This was not the jersey he wore during play—note the sleeve number 15. Gretzky wore 99 in Indianapolis, as he throughout his storied career.

The lineup insert from the program in Wayne Gretzky's first professional game, October 14, 1978, against the Winnepeg Jets at Market Square Arena. The Jets' lineup featured hockey legend Bobby Hull. Winnipeg won the game 6-3, with Willy Lindstrom scoring the game-winning goal. (Courtesy of the Spade collection.)

YOUR CENTRAL INDIANA AMC DEALERS PRESENT TONIGHT'S LINE-UP

Racers vs. Winnipeg

SATURDAY, OCTOBER 14, 1978

GOALTENDERS				GOALTENDERS		
1	GARY SMITH	G		1	JOE DALEY	G
30	GARY INNESS	G		35	MARKUS MATTSSON	G
31	EDDIE MIO	G				
DEFENSEMEN				**DEFENSEMEN**		
2	DAVE INKPEN	D		2	MIKE AMODEO	D
3	GLEN IRWIN	D		3	BARRY LONG	D
4	KEVIN MORRISON	D		5	KIM CLACKSON	D
5	JOHN HUGHES	D		6	TED GREEN	D
6	AL McLEOD	D		7	SCOTT CAMPBELL	D
24	KEN BLOCK	D		23	PAUL TERBENCHE	D
	JERRY ROLLINS	D		24	PAUL MacKINNON	D
				25	BILL DAVIS	D
FORWARDS				**FORWARDS**		
7	BLAINE STOUGHTON	RW		8	TERRY RUSKOWSKI	C
8	RENE LECLERC	RW		9	BOBBY HULL	LW
9	CLAUDE LAROSE	LW		10	PETER SULLIVAN	C
10	RICHIE LEDUC	C		11	KENT NILSSON	C
12	KEVIN NUGENT	RW		12	MORRIS LUKOWICH	LW
15	DON BURGESS	C		14	DALE YAKIWCHUK	C
16	MICHEL PARIZEAU	C		15	GLENN HICKS	LW
17	BRUCE GREIG	LW		16	JOHN GRAY	LW
20	CLAUDE ST. SAUVEUR	C		17	BILL LESUK	LW
21	DON LARWAY	RW		18	BOB GUINDON	LW
23	PETER DRISCOLL	LW		20	WILLY LINDSTROM	RW
25	ANGIE MORETTO	C		21	RICH PRESTON	RW
99	WAYNE GRETZKY	C		22	LYLE MOFFAT	LW
				26	STEVE WEST	C
COACH: PAT STAPLETON				COACH: LARRY HILLMAN		

Next Racer Home Game
Sun., Oct. 15 with Birmingham

Wayne Gretzky's jersey hangs in the Hockey Hall of Fame in Toronto.

Pat Stapleton joined the team during the 1975–76 season and quickly became a fan favorite. Seen here, patrolling the blue line in Quebec, "Whitey" was a steady presence and one of the team's leaders during its run to the East Division title in 1976. The Racers made both of their postseason appearances in Stapleton's two years in Indianapolis. He joined the Cincinnati Stingers in 1977–78, but returned to coach the Racers in their final season.

FIVE

Checking In

CHECKERS 1979–1987

By the time 1979 rolled around, the events leading up to the Indianapolis Racers' midseason demise left a bitter taste tainting hockey in Indianapolis.

But the Racers had built some momentum during their tenure—after all, 1979 was only two years removed from the team's glory days playing postseason games to packed houses.

As summer wound on, there were rumblings the Central Hockey League—a 16-year-old circuit one step removed from the NHL—would place a team in Indianapolis. Jerry Buss, who controlled the Market Square Arena, wanted a team. The CHL was filling all the old World Hockey Association markets—Birmingham, Cincinnati, and Houston were also slated for teams in the 1979–80 season.

On August 1, the Fort Worth Texans franchise transferred to Indianapolis. It was operated by, and affiliated with, the New York Islanders. Bert Marshall was named coach. Islanders president Bill Torrey addressed the bitter taste, saying, "[W]hen hockey treats Indianapolis right, Indianapolis will treat hockey right." There was debate about whether to call the team the Racers. It would be called the Checkers instead, it was decided, with the Islanders' blue and orange adopted for their top affiliate's colors.

The new era began October 10 with meeting with an old acquaintance, the Cincinnati Stingers—a descendent of the Racers' old World Hockey Association rival. The match began with a bang. Just 49 seconds in, Bruce Andres got into the franchise's first round of fisticuffs. At the 2:16 mark, Ed Pizunski scored the first goal in the new team's history on assists from Garth MacGuigan and Kevin Devine. Charlie Skjodt followed with the game-winner. Jim Park, a former Racer, allowed just one goal and the Checkers rolled in to an 8-1 victory.

It is fitting that Devine and MacGuigan assisted on the first-ever Checkers goal. Devine was the team's leader and captain, and he would retire having played more games in an Indianapolis uniform than anyone. He was a scrappy winger who could score, fight, and take care of a lot of the team's dirty work. MacGuigan was once called "the perennial Checker" in a program article, and was one of the team's leading scorers. Another fixture was Darcy Regier, a stalwart on defense who went on to coach the Checkers and eventually became the general manager of the NHL's Buffalo Sabres.

"Devine and MacGuigan were the key to our team. They were leaders on and off the ice," said Ron Handy, who joined the team as a rookie in 1982–83. "They really took the young guys under their wing and made us feel included. That's what made them champions. They treated everyone like family, and when everyone went on the ice, we didn't want to let them down.

"With Darcy, I was the wild child, and he was older. He showed me the ropes. He was my roommate on the road. He'd say, 'You're young, but you can't go out and party every night. This is your job. You can't lose it.' He was a smart defenseman. He wasn't the fastest guy, but you never saw him overcommit to things. He made sure he got the puck to the right people. You can see it now. He's got one heck of a career."

The Islanders believed in player development, but they were a budding NHL dynasty with a roster that would barely change over the next four years. They would win the first of four consecutive Stanley Cups in the 1979–80 season—their first year as the Checkers' parent club—and used many of the Indianapolis players for insurance. It led to a continuity in the roster almost unheard-of in minor-league hockey. MacGuigan, Devine, Regier, and Tim Lockridge played the next five seasons in Checker blue and orange.

"The Isles had so many good players," Handy said. "They were winning Stanley Cups. We were winning CHL Cups. Those players were really good. Many of them could've played in the NHL, but the league was smaller then, and if you signed a three-year contract, you were stuck with a team."

The Checkers had an impressive debut—they went 40-32-7 their first season and finished second in the league. They dominated the Tulsa Oilers in the first round of the playoffs, winning the three games by a combined score of 14-4, but ran into the team that replaced them in Fort Worth in the second round. The Texans ousted the Checkers in four games.

Although the Checkers were disappointed about the early exit, the Islanders were thrilled with the results—the superb on-ice season and a steady fan base built in the stands. Alex McKendry led the team with 40 goals. Devine scored 27 goals and was named team MVP.

Many of the same faces would be back for the 1980–81 season, with a new goaltender—20-year-old prospect Roland Melanson, who would soon play his way into the NHL. They'd also add Bruce Affleck, who was the CHL's top defenseman with Dallas the year before, and rookie Steve Stoyanovich.

They would pay off with a stellar season. The Checkers were 19-19-2 the first half of the season, which featured several trades and roster changes, but rolled through the second half, setting a CHL record with 12 straight wins. By the end of the year, Melanson was an Islander and the Checkers had picked up goaltender Rob Holland from the Pittsburgh Penguins—who would become a mainstay in blue and orange the rest of his career.

Holland was in goal when the Checkers opened the postseason against the Wichita Wind and backstopped a split of the first two games. Going on the road, Marshall inserted Kelly Hrudey, a rookie who had spent the entire season in junior hockey, in goal for Game 3 of a playoff series. The 19-year-old made 28 saves, and the Checkers won 4-2 in his high-pressure professional debut. Wichita rallied to win Game 4 and ended up taking the series in the deciding fifth game, when CHL leading goal scorer Tom Roulston scored on a long slap shot in overtime to give the Wind a 6-5 victory and the series win.

Marshall and Jim Devellano left the club after the season to take positions in the NHL. In their place was a well-respected, hard-drilling former NHL coach named Fred Creighton, a coaching veteran who had won an Adams Cup in 1973. The hiring of Creighton would be a huge change. The hard-nosed coach would lead the Checkers to even greater on-ice success, with two Adams Cup titles and an unexpected Adams Cup Finals appearance in his three full seasons as the team's coach.

"He was as tough as they got," Hrudey said of Creighton. "He'd always put on the wall what our championship ring would look like and left it up there. He was hard-nosed. But when it was all said and done, he was the first guy to start the party. Fred was like going back to the old school."

Creighton's era started slowly, but the Checkers picked up steam at mid-season. The

Checkers made a big move going into the 1981–82 season, signing free-agent Red Laurence, one of the CHL's top scorers with Salt Lake. He had won two straight Adams Cup titles and would lead the Checkers in scoring the next two seasons. He turned out to be the final piece in the championship puzzle on a team that retained its core—Garth MacGuigan, Neil Hawryliw, Glen Duncan, Kelly Davis, Darcy Regier, Kevin Devine, Tim Lockridge, Charlie Skjodt, Monty Trottier, Rob Holland, and Kelly Hrudey were all back for that season.

On March 12, Hrudey blanked Salt Lake 5-0 to end a four-year-old scoring streak by the Golden Eagles, helping the Checkers finish 42-33-5. He did it to the Tulsa Oilers three weeks later to open the playoffs. The Chex disposed of Tulsa in three games, then opened the semifinals in front of 12,000 fans in Edmonton, as the Wichita Wind's home rink was unavailable. Devine redirected a shot by Hawryliw with 1:25 to go, giving the Chex a 3-2 victory and setting the stage for a four-game sweep and a visit to the Adams Cup Finals against the Dallas Black Hawks. The Checkers won their eighth straight in Game 1, rallied from a two-goal deficit to win Game 3, and took a commanding 3-1 lead when Laurence scored 2:25 into double-overtime to win Game 4 by a 3-2 score. Their celebration was delayed by a day, but they finished off the championship in Game 6, with Laurence scoring two second-period goals to lead a 5-1 Adams Cup-clinching victory in front of 6,423 fans. Laurence finished the playoffs with 11 goals, while Hrudey was named playoff MVP with an 11-2 record in the playoffs.

It set the stage for what would be a special year. Nearly everyone was back, including the goaltending tandem of Holland and Hrudey. Laurence remained a scoring machine—totaling 43 goals and 55 assists for the second straight year. The Checkers finished 50-28-2 and ran away with the league title—even though they lost 14 straight road games at midseason. They swept nearly every postseason award, with Holland and Hrudey winning the top goaltender trophy, Hrudey the league MVP, Gord Dineen the top defenseman and most improved defenseman and Laurence the Ironman award.

The postseason pitted the league's two most powerful franchises against one another—Indianapolis and Salt Lake. Newcomer Scott Howson scored a hat trick in Game 1, including the game-winner 6:08 into overtime to get the Checkers rolling to a six-game series win.

"We were losing 2-1, and Fred Creighton looked to me with 1:30 left in the game and asked, 'Can you play right wing?' I went in, played right wing and tied the game up. We went into overtime and Scott Howson and I went on a two-on-one, and I slid the puck to Scotty and he scored," Handy said.

The Checkers finished it with a convincing 11-4 victory in Game 6, with Laurence scoring his second hat trick of the series and the team setting a CHL record for goals scored. The final series used an unusual best-of-nine format and saw the Checkers lose two of the first three games to the Birmingham South Stars. The series changed in Game 4, when Laurence took the puck off a faceoff and scored on a long slap shot with one second left in overtime to give the Checkers a 5-4 victory. They rolled to win the next three games 5-2, 3-2 and 7-2 and took the Adams Cup. The Chex scored five unanswered goals in the second and third periods of Game 7, including a hat trick by Glen Duncan, and Bruce Affleck was named the playoff MVP with 13 assists.

"We were skating around the rink, and people were throwing stuff at us, yelling, 'You should've stayed in junior,'" said Handy, who was a rookie that season. "It was a big thrill to win."

"Everybody says the second isn't as sweet as the first," Hrudey said in a Checkers program story. "That's a farce. It's better. Everybody is just waiting for you to fail, and to win again, it's just a great feeling."

The Checkers' run to a third Adams Cup title seemed to be unlikely after several players left. Davis and Randy Johnston retired; Hrudey and Gord Dineen moved up to the NHL, and several rookies took their places. They opened the 1984–85 season in front of 6,713 fans against the U.S. Olympic Team—whose interest had been piqued four years earlier by the Miracle on Ice. The Olympians won 4-3. One of the mainstays—Regier, one of several Checkers back for his fifth season with the club—set a CHL record by playing in his 537th career game at midseason. The team finished fourth in a five-team league—one that was in jeopardy of folding. The Tulsa Oilers had been booted out of their rink at midseason, and two other teams were struggling. The Checkers were hardly a championship contender, especially when facing a Colorado Flames team that featured future NHLer Mike Vernon in goal. But when the Checkers challenged the Flame saying that the curve on Pierre Rioux's stick was illegal, they won the challenge and scored on the ensuing power play with 1:34 to go in Game 5, and the series changed. Devine scored 58 seconds into overtime to beat the shell-shocked Flames 6-5. Laurence scored twice in Game 6 to lead a 3-2 victory and finish the upset in six games.

The former Tulsa team—now known as just "The Oilers"—would be the other finalist. Without a home for the Oilers, the entire Adams Cup series would be played in Indianapolis. But the Checkers suffered a serious blow when Holland suffered an injury in the Colorado series. Backup Todd Lumbard stepped into goal and stared down the ice at future NHL regular John Vanbiesbrouck. By the time Holland was healthy, the Checkers trailed 3-0. Game 4 had to be played in the Carmel Ice Skadium due to the unavailability of both the Coliseum and Market Square Arena. It was a fitting site for a homeless team to win the final championship of a soon-to-be-defunct league. Oiler defenseman Grant Ledyard scored an unassisted goal six minutes into the third period to give his team enough cushion in a 3-2 Adams Cup-clinching victory.

It would mark the end of the CHL, whose demise came swiftly after the season. Indianapolis and Salt Lake, the league's two most solvent franchises, were invited into the International Hockey League, at the time a Midwest-based bus league. The Fort Wayne Komets—who once sent players to the Checkers—would become their biggest rival.

The Islanders relinquished ownership and a group led by Indianapolis businessman Al Savill took over. Creighton became the team's general manager, Darcy Regier was named coach and a handful of former CHL checkers—MacGuigan, Devine, Lockridge, Charlie Skjodt and Holland among them—formed the core of the team. The Minnesota North Stars and Boston Bruins joined the Isles as parent clubs.

The Checkers won their IHL opener 7-0 against Fort Wayne, giving fans hopes the new era would feature the same runaway success the team had already enjoyed. But it wouldn't be the case. Regier wouldn't make it through the season—ousted in late March in favor of Moe Bartoli, a move that angered fans. The team finished 31-44-7, the first sub-.500 record in its history. Skjodt led the team in scoring with 33 goals and 67 points. The team endured another coaching change when Creighton replaced Bartoli with himself after the team lost Game 1 of its playoff series against the Peoria Rivermen. Immediately, the Checkers rallied to win three of the next four games and move to the brink of victory. Peoria won the final two to claim the series.

The team received a major overhaul entering 1985-86. Carmel businessman Larry Woods purchased the team, named Ron Ullyot coach and general manager, introduced a new logo and moved it back to Market Square Arena. The roster also went through a major overhaul, as Skjodt, Trottier and Holland were the only CHL holdovers left. Mike Zanier took the No. 1 goaltending job and led the Chex to a 41-35-6 record. Lakso scored an overtime goal to give the Checkers a Game 1 victory in their first-round series against Muskegon, but the Lumberjacks won the next four games to oust the Checkers.

While many of the old CHL mainstays were gone, Lakso became one on the IHL side. He scored 228 points in three years with the team, playing in each of its IHL seasons.

"He was one of the best left wings I ever played with. He was so fast, and had one accurate wrist shot. He didn't have a slap shot, but he didn't need it. He'd get open on the left wing, and I knew if I could get him the puck, he'd score," Handy said.

Handy returned to the team in 1986-87 as a 23-year-old and put together an amazing year, totaling 55 goals, 80 assists and 135 points. He had just been cut loose from the Islanders organization and signed with the Checkers as a free agent.

"It was the kind of year where I went out there to prove myself. It was a lot of fun. It was a time when you negotiated your own contracts, and there wasn't a lot of money," Handy said. "I

56

went to our owner and said, 'What would you give me if I had 100 points? He said, 'For 100 points, I'll give you $1,000.' 'I said, fine, what about every point over 100.' He said, 'for every point over 100, I'll give you $25 a point.' But I made him pay. It was a good experience going back there."

That season, the Minnesota North Stars and New Jersey Devils would supply players to the Checkers—ending the Islanders' seven-year affiliation with the club—and Ullyot returned as coach to provide stability. But a six-game loss to the IHL regular-season champion Fort Wayne Komets in the postseason ousted the Checkers in the first round for the third straight year.

The team's motto that season was "On the road to the NHL"—making no bones about its hopes to move up in the hockey world. Woods said the team needed to average 6,000 fans per game to attract the NHL's attention and award Indy a big-league franchise. Instead, the Checkers were on the road to extinction. Although the North Stars had indicated a desire to affiliate with the Checkers for the next season, they instead joined the Kalamazoo Wings. Woods attempted to sell the team but was unsuccessful in finding buyers. On Aug. 10, IHL commissioner Bud Poile said the team would be put into suspension, quietly ending the Checkers' eight-year run. It had been on the decline since the glory days of the CHL, when they enjoyed the double pleasure of runaway success and roster stability—two things difficult to put together in the minors. The change of their final three years was too much to keep it afloat.

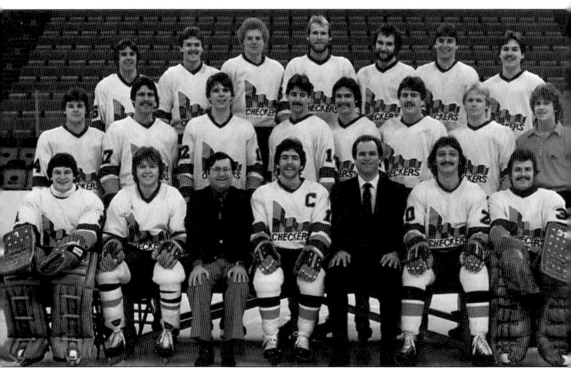

The 1980-81 Checkers, their second season, from left to right, are pictured as follows: (front row) Roland Melanson, Charlie Skjodt, general manager Jim Devellano, captain Kevin Devine, coach Bert Marshall, Hector Marini, and Jim Park; (second row) Glen Duncan, Bruce Affleck, Dave Cameron, Alex Pirus, Garth MacGuigan, Tim Lockridge, Darcy Regier, and trainer Craig Smith; (back row) Lorne Stamler, Shane Turner, Mike Hordy, Randy Johnston, Neil Hawryliw, Billy Carroll, and Kelly Davis. (Courtesy of the Spade collection.)

Charlie Skjodt graces the cover of the team's 1980–81 media guide. Skjodt later worked in the team's front office. His younger brother, Paul Skjodt, bought the Indianapolis Ice in 2004. The Ice are a direct descendant of the Checkers.

The Checkers made a number of changes in 1981–82. They moved to the Fairgrounds Coliseum and hired Fred Creighton to be the team's coach and general manager. The result was the club's first Central Hockey League Adams Cup championship. Team members, from left to right, are pictured as follows: (front row) Rob Holland, John Marks, captain Kevin Devine, coach/GM Fred Creighton, Lorne Stamler, and Kelly Hrudey; (middle row) assistant trainer George Schmitt, Neil Hawryliw, Randy Johnston, Charlie Skjodt, Steve Stoyanovich, Mats Hallin, Kelly Davis, Garth MacGuigan, Tim Lockridge, trainer Don Niederkorn; (back row) Glen Duncan, Frank Beaton, Darcy Regier, Bruce Andres, Mike Hordy, Monty Trottier, and Red Laurence. (Courtesy of the Spade collection.)

The Checkers won another championship in 1982–83, winning 50 games and beating the Birmingham South Stars 5-2 in the best-of-nine final. The Checkers, from left to right, are pictured as follows: (front row) Rob Holland, Darcy Regier, coach/GM Fred Creighton, captain Kevin Devine, Lorne Stamler, and Kelly Hrudey; (middle row) assistant trainer Scott Wyland, Glen Duncan, Kelly Davis, Tim Lockridge, Mats Hallin, Dave Hanson, Mike Greeder, Garth MacGuigan, Steve Stoyanovich, and trainer Don Niederkorn; (back row) Red Laurence, Randy Johnston, Scott Howson, Dave Simpson, Gord Dineen, Greg Gilbert, and Monty Trottier. (Courtesy of the Spade collection.)

$1.25

the**CHECKER FLAG**

1983-84 SOUVENIR PROGRAM

This program cover from the 1983–84 season depicts the championship rings won by the team the previous year. (Courtesy of the Indianapolis Checkers.)

Kevin Devine hoists the Adams Cup after the 1982–83 season. The Checkers beat Birmingham 7-2 in the final game of the finals to win their second straight championship. (Courtesy of the Indianapolis Checkers.)

KEVIN DEVINE

INDIANAPOLIS CHECKERS

82-83

INDIANAPOLIS
CHECKERS ®

Kevin Devine was the Indianapolis Checkers' perennial captain and a fixture on the team. In six seasons with the Checkers and another with the Racers, Devine played 542 games, more than any other professional hockey player in Indianapolis. He totaled 158 goals and 194 assists in that span. He is pictured here on one of the hockey cards the team released.

Tim Lockridge was another fixture on the Checkers roster. A defenseman, Lockridge played 393 games with the Checkers from 1979 to 1986—playing every season with the team except the final one. He was a key component of both championship teams. (Courtesy of the Indiana State Fairgrounds.)

Goaltender Rob Holland, seen here with Tim Lockridge, twice shared the CHL's top goaltender award with teammate Kelly Hrudey and helped lead the Checkers to the 1982 and 1983 championships. (Courtesy of the Indianapolis Checkers.)

1986-87 Season Schedule

ADAMS CUP CHAMPS!

ON THE ROAD TO NHL

Checkers

Games Times:
Monday- Sunday ...... 7:30 p.m.
Friday .... 8:00 p.m.
Unless Otherwise Announced

1982-83 INDIANAPOLIS CHECKERS SCHEDULE

A collage of two Checkers schedules—one from the 1982–83 season, declaring the team Adams Cup champions. The other comes from 1986–87, the team's final season, in which it pushed to be recognized as a potential NHL expansion club. The team instead went into suspension at the end of the year and never iced another game. Also pictured is a ticket from the Checkers' first-ever game.

Ron Handy returned to the team for the 1986–87 season and totaled a club-record 135 points, with 55 goals and 80 assists. He was named a second-team All-Star for his efforts. (Courtesy of the Indianapolis Ice.)

Bob Lakso totaled 228 points in three seasons with the Checkers. While players like Garth MacGuigan, Kevin Devine, Rob Holland, and Darcy Regier were the "face" of the Checkers in their CHL era, Lakso became so during their IHL era. He played in each of the team's three IHL seasons. (Courtesy of the Indianapolis Ice.)

SIX
Revival on Ice
ICE 1988–1999

For sixteen years, the name "Ice" was synonymous with hockey in Indianapolis. That tradition officially began in a Montreal boardroom on June 9, 1988, when the International Hockey League's governors approved the sale of the Indianapolis Checkers from Larry Woods to Chicago businessman Horn Chen—the first of an extensive number of sports teams that would make up Chen's portfolio.

A month later, in the midst of an oppressive heat wave, the name "Ice" was chosen along with the black-and-silver team colors. That day, a local television sportscaster brought a large block of ice onto his sports report.

The seeds of the Ice image were sowed. The front-office staff was a group of people who knew very little about hockey, but knew how to entertain—creating a personality that led to a decade and a half of off-the-wall stunts and wacky promotions—tie-dyed jerseys for "IceStock," Elvis impersonators, pink jerseys on Valentine's Day, wrestling midgets, and nights recognizing everything from the Gong Show to the Brady Bunch. Those promotions became as much a part of the team's image in Indianapolis as the kick saves and slapshots on the ice, as the team developed a reputation for giving an honest evening's entertainment and doing just about anything to get people in the door for a hockey game.

Many were the brainchild of Ray Compton, a former newspaper reporter and Indiana Pacers executive who was named the team's first general manager. He and sidekicks Roy Hurley and David Paitson had barely seen hockey when October 7, 1988 rolled around—the day of the Ice's first game against the Peoria Rivermen. Their newness showed when there was no organ to provide in-rink entertainment—a move the front office heard quite a bit about that night and quickly fixed. They didn't know what to expect when they got to the Fairgrounds Coliseum.

What they saw were fans lined up out the door—6,502 in all. Some didn't get in until the second period.

"We put things together so quickly," Compton said. "We started the team at the end of June, and at the first of October, we were playing. None of us really knew what we were doing. We didn't know if there were going to be 1,500 people at the game. There were 7,000 and people were lined up. We were crying. We were happy."

Things got off to a bit of an ignominious start, even aside from there being no organ. For one thing, there were the introductions. "Ray had gotten some kids to line up and make a tunnel for us. There was a bunch of smog, and through it, I came tearing out onto the ice, all excited, and ran over about four kids," Ice player Ron Handy said.

Peoria won the game 4-3, but a tradition was born. The first team put up the worst record in the franchise's history—26-54-2—but remained memorable for its personality. The team colors of black and silver were chosen to emulate those of the Oakland Raiders. The team was supposed to take on the same aggressive, hard-hitting attitude. Former NHL tough guy Archie Henderson was the coach, and the team set a professional hockey record with 3,067 penalty minutes—an average of 37 minutes a game. Twelve different players amassed over 100 minutes, led by Jimmy Mann's 275 in just 38 games.

"We had a lot of characters, but we all got along great in the dressing room," Handy said. "Everybody gave 110 percent every night, but we didn't have much talent. We had myself, (Brent) Sapergia and (Bob) Lakso to score goals, but we took so many penalties; it's tough to score when you're killing penalties. Archie and I got into it one night. We had lost 4-2, and he said, 'If you, Sapergia, and Lakso would've scored, we'd have won the game.' I said, 'Coach, if we weren't killing off 200 minutes of penalties, we would've won.' One thing, we intimidated other teams. A lot of teams didn't like to come to our rink and play us."

Handy was the Ice's leading scorer that season, tallying 100 points. Sapergia added 43 goals in just 52 games.

But things soon changed. In the summer of 1989, the Chicago Blackhawks announced the Ice would be their IHL affiliate. Compton later called the move the team's "lottery pick." It began a 10-year relationship between the two franchises. The honeymoon period was just that.

Out was the hastily put together team of tough guys. In was coach Darryl Sutter and a veteran crew full of top-line prospects. Brian Noonan, Warren Rychel, Mike Peluso, Mike Eagles, and Bob Bassen would go on from that team to spend a significant amount of time in the NHL. Capitan Jim Playfair would later assist Sutter as a coach in the NHL. In addition, players like forward Sean Williams and Jim Johannson and defensemen Ryan McGill and Bruce Cassidy played key roles. The centerpiece was the backstop, Jim Waite, a young All-Star goaltender who would prove tough to beat.

"We had great talent and veteran leadership," Williams said. "Just as importantly, we had a coach who kept us committed. Sometimes in the minors, you get players who aren't as committed, but our goal was to win a championship from Day 1. We had a great mix of players. We had good goaltending, the right amount of veterans, solid defensemen, guys who could score. We worked together. It provided the right chemistry."

The Ice lost their first four games, but they'd be difficult to beat after that. In October and November, they won 10 of 11 games, shot to the West Division lead and never relinquished it. They clinched the title so early, the division championship banner was hanging over the Coliseum rink long before the season ended. But that wouldn't be the only banner. Late in the season, Mike Stapleton and goaltender Darren Pang joined the team to add some late punch. The Ice finished the regular season with a 53-21-8 record—still a franchise best—but they weren't finished there.

The Ice dispatched of the Peoria Rivermen in five games, clinching when Johannson scored the game-winner to beat the Rivermen 3-2 in the Coliseum. Noonan's overtime goal in Game 5 of the next series clinched a victory over the Salt Lake Golden Eagles, setting up a best-of-7 affair for the Turner Cup with the powerful Muskegon Lumberjacks, who had taken six of eight meetings with the Ice during the regular season.

Waite backstopped 5-2 wins in Games 1 and 2 to give the Ice an early lead. Mike McNeill scored an overtime goal to give Indy a 5-4 win in Game 3, bringing the series back to the Coliseum for a chance to clinch. On that Monday night, 6,003 broom-waving Ice fans descended on the rink—the largest home Coliseum playoff crowd in franchise history—to see a potential championship victory. The home team didn't disappoint. With Waite and

Muskegon's Chris Clifford both playing well, goals would be difficult to come by. Which is why, when Eagles banged a rebound home 5:43 into the second period, the rafters began to shake. And when Williams—who had assisted on Eagles' goal—took a behind-the-net feed from Mike Rucinski, got Clifford off-balance and scored—everyone began to smell a championship. The Ice, after all, were unbeaten when leading going into the third period. They had to sweat out a one-goal lead—Muskegon had scored with 34 seconds left in the second—but Waite and the defense stood up to every challenge. And eventually, the fans were standing on their seats, counting down the seconds, and a mass of white, black and silver was in a pile at center ice, awaiting the tall, tiered Turner Cup. Several observers said the crowd at the end of the game was the loudest they'd ever heard in any arena.

"It came down to the wire," Williams said. "We had a great crowd for a Monday. The players were extremely excited. Anytime you can win a championship at a level like the IHL, it's pretty exciting, especially when you play with great players."

"They just had the attitude that they weren't going to get beat," Stapleton added. "They could be down 5-0 and not be worried about it."

To show how deep and balanced the Ice were, the Turner Cup MVP went to Mike McNeill, who had just 10 points in 14 playoff games, but provided toughness and leadership.

Interestingly, the Ice lost the Turner Cup as quickly as they had won it. During a week-long celebration, the Cup turned up missing. The Cup apparently was left on a sidewalk—where someone else was supposed to pick it up. It wasn't seen again for several weeks but eventually turned up.

With new leadership, the Ice continued strong in 1990-91. Noonan, Stapleton, Johannson, Williams, Rychel, Eagles, Waite, Cam Russell and Ryan McGill returned to play for new coach Dave MacDowall. Also, a backup goaltender named Dominik Hasek joined the team from the Czech Republic that year.

"Chicago always provided us with great goaltenders," Williams said. "Waite, Hasek, Darren Pang (who played in 1989–90) and Ray LeBlanc were all very good."

The Ice finished strong once again, going 48-29-5 and finishing second to Muskegon in the East Division. That meant a first-round pairing with the arch-rival Fort Wayne Komets. The teams battled through an epic series, which saw five of the seven games decided by a goal. The teams held serve in the first four games, with Martin Desjardins scoring an overtime goal in Game 1 and Noonan scoring late in Game 3 to preserve Ice wins at home. But in Game 5, the Komets skated away with a 2-1 win. MacDowall went with Dominik Hasek in Game 6 in Fort Wayne.

"We went up to Fort Wayne, and their crowd is pretty raucous, especially for Indianapolis," Williams said. "We put Hasek in net and he stood on his head. We got a couple of power-play goals and won the game."

The score was 4-3, as Hasek and the Ice survived a late flurry to send the series to a seventh game. The teams skated to a 3-3 tie in the opening periods, but the Komets got an odd bounce and won the game in sudden-death overtime.

"We had momentum. Unfortunately, we got to overtime and they got a lucky bounce," Williams said.

The roster saw several new players for 1991–92 and another new coach in former Checker John Marks. Williams and Stapleton were back and Brad Lauer joined the team, but the Ice won just 31 games and failed to make the playoffs. It wasn't for the lack of trying—Ray LeBlanc returned from the Olympics in mid-February, where he had backstopped the United States on an incredible run to the semifinals. He remained hot upon returning to Indy, stepping in and leading a streak in which the Ice won 12 of 13 games, one of the most incredible goaltending streaks in team history. He finished it with back-to-back shutouts of Milwaukee and Fort Wayne.

In 1992-93, the Ice were back in the playoffs, due in large part to the play of Tony Hrkac, who scored 45 goals and had 87 assists for a franchise-record 132-point season.

He didn't just make an impression on the ice, either.

"Tony Hrkac was amazing. Just his professionalism, his demeanor, his attitude toward the game," said Kevin St. Jacques, who was an Ice rookie then. "I remember my first road trip, I roomed with Hrkac. We just sat there, had a bag of popcorn and a soda. I looked at him and said, 'Wow. This is big-time now.'"

The Ice eventually fell in five games to the Atlanta Knights in the postseason, playing all their home games at Market Square Arena. They eventually liked the place so much, the franchise moved to the hockey-friendly building for the 1994-95 season. In typical Ice flair, Compton announced the move by inviting the local media to a press conference, then driving them to MSA to "announce" it. In addition, purple was added to the black and silver, creating the color scheme the Ice used from then on.

After missing the playoffs in three of the previous four years, the Ice's fortunes began to change with the hiring of Bob Ferguson as coach in 1995–96. With Ferguson's hiring came some key new players—high-scoring forwards James Black and Kip Miller and versatile defensemen Brad Werenka among them. Waite, who had been acquired from the San Jose Sharks at the end of the 1994–95 season, was also back. They brought a new attitude to the Ice, and new success. The biggest night of the year came on March 9, 1996, when 14,631 fans crammed into MSA for Pack The House Night against Fort Wayne. After a 2-1 shootout win, the Ice players skated back onto the rink to acknowledge the thrilled crowd. Another highlight came on December 26, when Waite stopped a flurry of late shots in Cincinnati in a memorable clutch performance. The 2-1 Ice win was beamed back to Indy viewers on TV, as WNDY televised several games that season.

Crowds began to grow at MSA, with the team's wild promotions taking center stage. One night, the team dressed up in tie-dyed jerseys and celebrated "IceStock," a return to the 1960s that received national attention in USA Today. On another, they wore pink jerseys with red hearts on Valentine's Day. Many promotions centered around the team's rivalry with Fort Wayne. The Ice staged a hug-in with Fort Wayne fans one night and passed out "Komets make me vomit" signs on another. It was all in an effort to keep the team front-and-center in an increasingly crowded market. It also was an attempt to introduce hockey to a new set of potential fans.

"We had to come up with ways that would make us come to the games," Compton said. "By doing that, we thought we could get more of the public involved in hockey. I think it worked."

The Ice finished with a 43-33-6 mark and nearly pulled an upset of the powerful Detroit Vipers in the opening round of the playoffs, taking the first two games 3-2 and 3-0 in Detroit. But the Vipers won three close games to clinch the best-of-five series.

Werenka returned for 1996–97, but had a strong cast with him, led by fellow defenseman Chris Snell and forwards Dave Chyzowski and Steve Dubinsky. Gritty players like Craig Mills and Alain Nasreddine played a big role, as did smooth defenseman Christian LaFlamme, while Waite and Marc Lamothe shared time in goal. Miller was re-acquired at mid-season and Indiana native and NHL veteran Fred Knipscheer joined the team for the playoff drive. The net result was a 44-29-9 mark and the franchise's first division championship since 1990. Playoff disappointment followed, however. Despite splitting 6-3 games with the Cleveland Lumberjacks at MSA—Dubinsky had a hat trick in Game 1—the Jacks won a 2-1 Game 3 in Cleveland and then clinched the series when ex-Iceman Brad Lauer scored deep into the second OT in Game 4.

Rookie Todd White and Petri Varis led the Ice into the 1997–98 season, which saw the Ice recover from a slow start to finish 40-36-6. The Ice took the favored Orlando Solar Bears to the wire in their first-round playoff series, as White's OT goal in Game 4 brought the Ice close, but Orlando took the decisive Game 5.

Some big changes were in store for 1998–99. First, the Ice moved from MSA—their home of five years—back to the Pepsi Coliseum. Next, popular Ice alum Bruce Cassidy, who played with the team from the 1989–90 championship season until 1995–96, was named head coach. Another familiar face in Brian Noonan was on the roster. Dave Hymovitz had a breakout year with 46 goals, but the midseason acquisition of goaltender Geoff Sarjeant helped get the undermanned Ice into the playoff hunt at season's end.

That season, the Ice went "retro" to play the final hockey game at Market Square Arena. The team wore red Indianapolis Racers-style uniforms to honor MSA's first hockey tenant, as several ex-Racers attended the game and even former Racer Wayne Gretzky addressed the crowd on video before the game. Gretzky's No. 99 was hung from the rafters that night.

With their backs to the wall—one loss would eliminate them—the overachieving Ice won their last five games in hair-raising fashion to get into the playoffs. Four were on the road and three were won in shootouts. In the playoffs, they won two one-goal games to come from behind and win their first-round series with Cincinnati, before taking the powerful Detroit Vipers to their limit in the second round. Stan Drulia finally ended the Ice's run by scoring with six seconds left in Game 4 of their best-of-five series.

"That was a nice feeling," Cassidy said. "The pressure was on, but we were so loose. We kept coming from behind. The team kept believing in itself and rolled into the playoffs. They were a very resilient bunch."

In their final few years, the Ice's future became a bit cloudy. Chen claimed losses from each year he owned the team. Over the previous 11 years, the IHL went from a largely Midwestern base to an international circuit stretching from Quebec City to San Francisco. Bus rides to Muskegon were replaced by plane trips to San Antonio, while player salaries and operating costs began to escalate. The Blackhawks partially pulled their affiliation and began placing prospects in the American Hockey League in 1998–99, the same year the team moved back to the Coliseum. The IHL itself was hurtling toward an end that would come two years later. The Ice and Fort Wayne got out before it did, leaving the league within weeks of each other in June 1999. A new chapter would soon begin.

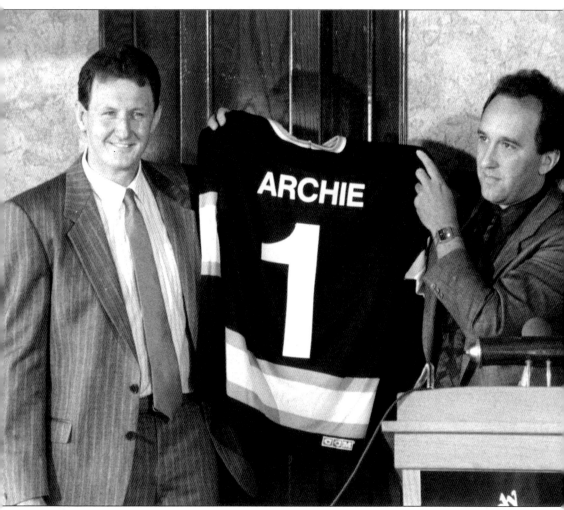

Archie Henderson (left) is given the No. 1 jersey symbolic of his being named the first head coach of the Indianapolis Ice. Ray Compton is presenting the jersey at Henderson's introduction. The Ice took on Henderson's rough-and-tumble personality that first year, setting professional hockey records for penalty minutes. In the front office, Compton set a tone for the Ice that would be followed by minor league teams across North America, using a variety of unusual promotions to sell hockey in the city. (Courtesy of the Indianapolis Ice.)

Mike Stapleton and Bob Bassen celebrate a goal during the 1989–90 season. Bassen was named "Mr. Ice" for his efforts in leading the team to the IHL West Division and Turner Cup championships that year. He had 54 points in 73 games, but was an important cog in the team. Stapleton joined the team late in the year and totaled 15 points in 16 games. Both were second-generation Indianapolis players. Stapleton's father was Pat "Whitey" Stapleton, who played for and coached the Indianapolis Racers in the 1970s. Bassen's father Hank was a goaltender for the Indianapolis Capitols in 1963. (Courtesy of the Indianapolis Ice.)

Goaltender Jim Waite turns aside a shot with Mike Eagles helping to clear the crease during a game at the Coliseum. Both players went on to play in the NHL. Waite became the face of the Ice, playing 217 games in goal in two stints—from 1989 to 1992, then again from 1994 to 1997. In the interim, he played with the San Jose Sharks. (Courtesy of the Indianapolis Ice.)

Bruce Cassidy (left) and Ryan McGill (right) congratulate goaltender Jimmy Waite during the 1989–90 season. Waite backstopped the Ice to nine wins in the Turner Cup playoffs, including a 2-1 victory in the final game that sealed a 4-0 Turner Cup Finals sweep of the Muskegon Lumberjacks. (Courtesy of the Indianapolis Ice.)

The Ice players celebrate moments after clinching the 1990 Turner Cup championship at the Coliseum. With 6,003 fans standing on their seats, the Ice won 2-1 to clinch the city's sixth professional hockey championship. (Courtesy of the Indianapolis Ice.)

Bruce Cassidy hoists the Turner Cup in 1990 with his Ice teammates trailing behind. Captain Jim Playfair is at the far left. (Courtesy of the Indianapolis Ice.)

Before going on to his record-setting NHL career, Dominik Hasek played parts of two seasons with the Ice from 1990 to 1992. In 53 games, he showed many of the skills that made him an Olympic gold medalist and Stanley Cup champion. His most memorable start came in Game 6 of the Ice's series with the Fort Wayne Komets in the 1991 playoffs. With the team facing elimination in a hostile environment, Hasek backstopped the Ice to a 4-3 victory and extended a memorable series to a seventh game. (Courtesy of the Indianapolis Ice.)

Sean Williams plays defense in a game at the Coliseum against the Muskegon Lumberjacks. Williams became the only member of the IHL Ice to have his number retired. He played 320 games with the team between 1989 and 1993, totaling 130 goals and 286 points. Williams helped lead the Ice to the 1990 Turner Cup championship. (Courtesy of the Indianapolis Ice.)

Defenseman Keith Carney was one of many Ice alumni who went on to long careers in the NHL. Carney played 28 games in Indianapolis in 1993–94 before moving up to Chicago. (Courtesy of the Indianapolis Ice.)

The Ice weren't bashful about wearing special uniforms to mark promotional nights. Above, five players model tie-dyed jerseys the team wore for "IceStock" in 1995–96. The evening played off a Woodstock theme and even garnered attention in USA Today. Below, James Black models a pink jersey adorned with hearts the team wore on Valentine's Day 1996. Black was the team's second-leading scorer that year with 82 points. (Courtesy of the Indianapolis Ice.)

Brad Werenka and Chris Snell made up one of the IHL's top defensive pairings in the late 1990s. Werenka was named the IHL's top defenseman in 1996–97 and totaled 133 points in two seasons with the Ice. Snell was a second-team IHL All-Star the same year, his only year with the Ice. Together, they helped lead the team to the 1997 Central Division championship. (Courtesy of the Indianapolis Ice.)

Steve Dubinsky played 209 games with the Ice between 1993 and 1997, helping lead the team to a division championship in 1997. He totaled 155 points and 155 penalty minutes during that span, in which he also played several games in the NHL. (Courtesy of the Indianapolis Ice.)

Todd White was the Ice's big gun as a rookie in 1997–98, leading the team with 82 points before graduating to a successful NHL career. One of White's most memorable moments came in the 1998 playoffs against the Orlando Solar Bears, when he scored an overtime goal to extend the series to a Game 5. (Courtesy of the Indianapolis Ice.)

Brian Noonan (front right) and assistant coach Dale DeGray look for the puck during a game in the Ice's final IHL season. Noonan returned to the Ice in 1998–99 after a long stint in the NHL.

Ice goaltender Geoff Sarjeant makes a save on the Las Vegas Thunder March 20, 1999, as Bret Meyers (top), Chris Herperger (middle) and Dave Hymovitz move in to clear the rebound. The game was the final one at Market Square Arena, and saw the Ice wear uniforms that were replicas of those once worn by the Indianapolis Racers.

Chris Herperger shoots against the Orlando Solar Bears in 1998–99. Herperger totaled 48 points with the Ice while beginning a career that eventually led him to a long tenure in the NHL.

Dave Hymovitz splits two Orlando Solar Bears during the 1998–99 season. He was the team's leading scorer in its final IHL year, totaling 76 points.

SEVEN

The Next Century

ICE 1999–2004

For many years before the summer of 1999, Ice owner Horn Chen hinted at moving the team out of the International Hockey League and into one of the lower minor leagues that had mushroomed across North America. After the Ice moved to the Pepsi Coliseum in 1998, a league jump appeared to be the next shift.

And with Chen also having a financial interest in the Central Hockey League—whose headquarters shared office space with the Ice staff—a move seemed inevitable.

That move came in the summer of 1999, and it came to the CHL, a league whose footprint was largely based in the Central Plains and Sun Belt. Fans would have to get used to new opposing teams, and players would learn to love long road trips—the Ice's closest rivals were in Huntsville, Alabama and Memphis. It wasn't all they'd get used to. The team underwent a complete overhaul, with a new logo, a completely new roster of players, a new coach in Rod Davidson and even new ownership, as a group led by local car dealer Gary Pedigo purchased the team from Chen that summer.

And while the Ice played the majority of their home games at the Pepsi Coliseum, they also had a new playpen in Conseco Fieldhouse, a state-of-the-art 15,000-seat Downtown building, which had replaced Market Square Arena, and where the Ice would play six home games.

Davidson's first moves were to bring in defensemen Bernie John and Mike Berger to be the team's cornerstones and forwards Chris MacKenzie and Yvan Corbin to provide the scoring punch. The new era opened October 16 in Columbus, Georgia—the same place where the first season would end several months later. Lubos Krajcovic scored on a rebound to tally the new franchise's first goal, with Berger assisting. While there was talent, the Ice looked like an expansion team early. They sat in last place on New Year's Day. But that night, the Ice came from behind to beat the Topeka ScareCrows 3-2 in a shootout in the Coliseum, and the team's fortunes changed in a heartbeat.

The Ice went on to win seven straight, get over the .500 mark, and never look back. Come-from-behind wins were the norm. A "refuse-to-lose" attitude led to games like a 5-4 shootout win over San Antonio in Conseco Fieldhouse, which saw the Ice rally from an early two-goal deficit, or a game in Wichita in which the Ice trailed 5-1 going into the third, came back and won 7-6 in a shootout.

"Once we started winning and got on that roll, it was almost like we can't lose," John said. "We were down 5-1 in Wichita going into the third, and we said, 'We're going to win this game,' and we won it in a shootout. We had a bunch of confidence. We should've won a lot of games with the team we had. We had Corbin and MacKenzie, but what really helped us was our second line. We had a lot of depth."

The Ice won a CHL-record 13 straight home games in January and February, and were 21-11-1 after New Year's Day. Corbin and MacKenzie both finished the season with 127 points and shared CHL Most Valuable Player honors.

The Ice went into the CHL Playoffs on a roll, facing the gritty Tulsa Oilers in the first round. Peter Jas' OT goal in Game 1 helped spur the Ice to a 2-0 lead in the best-of-5, but Tulsa won two games handily in its building. In Game 4, Davidson made a change that helped set the Ice up the rest of the way, inserting Jamie Morris in net mid-game.

Morris got the call for Game 5 and got a shutout in his first pro playoff start. He didn't have to sweat too much, as the Ice rolled to a 7-0 win in one of the bloodiest games in CHL history. With the series over, Tulsa took out its frustrations in the third period, which saw multiple fights break out and 302 penalty minutes called in the third period alone. At one point, backup goaltender Benoit Thibert was the only player on the Ice bench.

The Ice advanced and swept the powerful Oklahoma City Blazers in three games, with Yvan Corbin providing late-game heroics in both Game 1 and Game 2. In Game 1, he broke a 2-2 tie with a goal in the last 10 seconds of regulation. In Game 2, he scored another late goal to give the Ice a 2-1 win.

Morris then backstopped a 3-1 series-clinching victory back at the Coliseum. He allowed just four goals in the three games.

"He stole the whole series for us against Oklahoma City. He had 40 shots a game and we swept them," John said of Morris. "It was kind of ironic that happened. [OKC coach Doug] Sauter made statements like 'if they didn't have the hot goalie, they wouldn't have won it.' That might have been the case, but goaltending does win you hockey games. That's what you need once in a while."

The win gave the Cinderella Ice a spot in the Miron Cup Finals against the Columbus Cottonmouths. The teams split the first four games, two in Columbus and two weekend OT thrillers in the Coliseum, before Columbus won Game 5 by a 1-0 score. With Morris and Frankie Ouellette both playing well, goals were hard to come by. Only twice in the entire series did a team score more than two regulation goals against either.

"I've never seen such good goaltending than in that series," John said. "Morris and Ouellette played unbelievable. If it had been any two other guys, it probably would've been high-scoring,"

The Ice needed to win both games in Columbus to win the Cup. They went down and blasted the Cottonmouths in Game 6 by a 5-2 score, setting up a winner-take-all Game 7. Blaz Emersic gave the Ice a big early boost with a first-period goal, while Morris continued to stifle every Columbus rush. Finally, Peter Jas scored an empty-netter to ice the game and the countdown was on.

"It was 3-0. I had the puck behind the net, looking at the clock counting down," John said. "They weren't coming hard. There was 10 seconds left. I was behind Jamie and said, 'Mo, Mo we've done it.' The first guy I hugged was Brad Beery. The next guy I went to was Rod Davidson, who brought me here. I went and jumped into the pile."

The celebration lasted the entire weekend, as the new team in the new league had gone from last place to the championship. Corbin and MacKenzie had big offensive years, but the hero was Morris, who came on from the backup role at mid-season to become the Playoff MVP.

"We did something pretty special. We went down to Columbus down one game with two to play," John said "We said, 'Let's just go down there and see what happens.' After we won Game 6, just talking to the guys, we knew we were going to win the last game. Their game to win was Game 6. They didn't want to go to a Game 7. That 1-0 game could've gone either way. That was a series."

But many of the players credited the Ice's multiple midseason acquisitions—Dan Villeneuve, Blaz Emersic, Taj Schaffnit, Jan Jas and Mike Torkoff. Most were brought in around Christmas.

"We had some key additions late," Morris said. "Dan Villeneuve came in at Christmas and left his family. That was a big sacrifice. Because we were such a close team, we said, 'Hey, let's prove to some people they made the wrong decision.' A lot of guys were castoffs from other teams. Guys just really jell."

The Ice gunned for a repeat in 2000–01 with many of the same faces—minus Berger, who retired and saw his No. 44 raised to the rafters—but the big story was Corbin's assault on the CHL record books. Corbin needed 38 games to score 50 goals—two short of the pro hockey record—and kept rolling in the second half of the season.

The Ice's promotional savvy continued in the season finale. Steven Kirkpatrick, who had muscular dystrophy, started a key game against the Huntsville Tornado in goal. The winner would go to the playoffs. Huntsville center Chris George fired a shot into the stick of Kirkpatrick—who was confined to a wheelchair—to begin the game. Among those in attendance were Gordie and Colleen Howe. Corbin scored his CHL-record 75th goal in that game to lead the ice to a 4-1 victory and the final Eastern Division playoff spot. As if it were a playoff game, the teams lined up to shake hands after it was over.

The postseason wouldn't last long, as the Ice were swept by the Memphis RiverKings in the opening round.

Major changes would come in the following season. Corbin was gone and MacKenzie would be traded to El Paso at mid-year, leaving John and Morris as the lone holdovers from the championship season. The CHL and Western Professional Hockey League merged in the summer of 2001, creating a 16-team league that had nine franchises in Texas. Pedigo and the Ice ownership attempted to move the team out of the CHL and into the more geographically-sensible United Hockey League, which housed a number of the Ice's old IHL rival cities—including Muskegon, Kalamazoo, Flint, and Fort Wayne. Instead, Chen repurchased the team and kept it in the CHL, where it would play three more seasons.

The Ice signed George from the now-defunct Huntsville Tornado to replace Corbin's scoring prowess. He had 44 goals and 32 assists, but the team struggled to stay out of the penalty box and stumbled to an 20-37-7 record, well out of the playoff race.

Davidson was fired and replaced by former NHL player Ken McRae in the summer of 2002. McRae instilled a disciplined, forechecking style and stressed solid defensive play. While the Ice's goal totals went down, the team's success on the ice translated into the Northern Conference regular-season title.

"He's a workaholic. He's at the rink all the time," Morris said of McRae that season. "He's got his computer with him all the time; he's always on the phone. He's done some great recruiting. He's good to the guys. He communicates really well."

The Ice went 39-16-9 his first season and picked up a number of key players along the way. Shawn Silver eased into the No. 1 goaltending job, posted a 2.21 GAA, had six shutouts, a 200-minute scoreless streak and won 29 games. The Ice also signed former IHL player Kevin St. Jacques, who totaled 22 goals and 56 assists, and added big scorer Jason Baird.

John led a 3-games-to-1 victory over the Amarillo Gorillas in the best-of-five conference semifinal series. He set a CHL playoff record with four assists in Game 4. The eventual champion Memphis RiverKings swept the Ice out of the playoffs in the conference finals.

John would return for his fifth season with the team—fourth as captain—in 2003–04 — again as one of the CHL's top defenseman. The lone player left from the championship team finished with 76 points—second on the team to Baird's 79—and led the Ice to an 37-23-4 record and another postseason berth. Those points boosted John's career numbers with the franchise to 301 games, 353 points and 91 goals and 262 assists. John set team records in every category except goals, where Yvan Corbin totaled 137 in his two seasons with the club.

The Ice would face the Bossier-Shreveport Mudbugs in the opening round of the playoffs and take the series to the five-game limit before succumbing 3-1 in the final game of the series.

It would soon be announced the game was the Ice's final one as a professional franchise. Just days after the postseason loss—before the CHL playoffs were even over—it was announced the Ice had been sold to former Checkers player and Carmel businessman Paul Skjodt. They would move to the junior-level United States Hockey League and be renamed the Indiana Ice.

The move brought an end to the 16-year run of the Ice as a professional franchise, from Archie Henderson through two leagues and two championship seasons. It also marked a beginning of a new era of hockey in Indianapolis.

The Ice's Eric Landry takes the center ice draw in Columbus, Georgia, to open the franchise's first game as a hockey team October 16, 1999. The Ice lost the game 4-2, despite Lubos Krajcovic scoring the first goal in franchise history. (Courtesy of the Indianapolis Ice.)

Ice goaltender Benoit Thibert is the first to greet Jamie Morris after Game 5 of the team's opening-round series against Tulsa. Morris backstopped a 7-0 Ice victory for his first playoff shutout. That game was also notable for the 302 penalty minutes in the third period. Morris would remain hot throughout the playoffs and would be named the Playoff MVP after the Ice won the CHL championship.

Ice forward Chris MacKenzie (# 19) finds himself in a stack of Columbus Cottonmouths during Game 5 of the 2000 Miron Cup Finals. Columbus goaltender Frankie Ouellette had MacKenzie's number that day, as he shut out the Ice 1-0, but Indianapolis would have the last laugh, winning the final two games. MacKenzie had a stellar first season with Indianapolis, totaling 127 points. He and teammate Yvan Corbin were named the league's co-Most Valuable Players.

The Ice skate off the bench in Columbus, Georgia as champions, having just clinched the 2000 Miron Cup title. The team had been in last place when 1999 turned into 2000, but caught fire during the second half of the season, and won the championship in a scintillating seven-game series. (Courtesy of the Indianapolis Ice.)

Because they won the championship on the road, the Ice returned to Indianapolis and held a celebration with the team's fans at Pan Am Plaza downtown. The players mingled with fans and skated around with the Miron Cup, as coach Rod Davidson does here.

The Ice players gather at center ice in Columbus to celebrate the Miron Cup championship. (Courtesy of the Indianapolis Ice.)

Jamie Morris dives to make a save against the Memphis RiverKings in 2001. He played three seasons with the team, posting a GAA of 3.42 and a record of 52-51-13. His most memorable moment came in the 2000 playoffs, when he went 8-3, posted a 1.63 goals against average and a .947 save percentage. Morris shut out Columbus 3-0 in Game 7 of the final series.

Yvan Corbin (right) is congratulated by teammates Dan Cousineau (center) and Ken Boone (left) after scoring a goal during his record-setting 2000–01 season. Corbin scored a CHL-record 75 goals that year, capping it off with the record tally in the season finale against the Huntsville Tornado. (Courtesy of the Indianapolis Ice.)

Gordie and Colleen Howe joined Indy Racing League drivers Sarah Fisher (far left) and Sam Hornish Jr. (second from left) at the season finale in 2000-01 to raise support for muscular dystrophy. That day, wheelchair-bound goaltender Steven Kirkpatrick—accompanied by the Howes—played nine seconds in goal for the Ice and made a save on a shot by Huntsville's Chris George. (Courtesy of the Indianapolis Ice.)

Ken McRae became the Ice's coach prior to the 2002–03 season and immediately instilled a disciplined, heavy-forechecking approach. It paid off, as the Ice won the Northern Division title in McRae's first year as coach, and posted winning records in both of his seasons with the team.

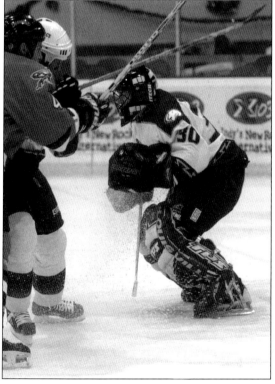

Ice goaltender Shawn Silver makes a save with players from Indianapolis and Bossier-Shreveport bearing down on him in 2002. Later that season, Silver posted a club-record 222:01-minute shutout streak that included two shutouts. It was the longest ever put together by an Indianapolis goaltender. He posted a 2.21 goals against average in the 2002–03 season and helped lead the Ice to the best record in their five-year CHL history.

The Ice's Kevin St. Jacques (16, left) digs for the puck in a game. St. Jacques was one of two former IHL Ice players to rejoin the team in its CHL era, being later joined by Mario Doyon. St. Jacques tallied a team-high 78 points on 22 goals and 56 assists in the 2002–03 season.

Ice winger Justin Kearns skates past a prone Amarillo player during a game at Conseco Fieldhouse in 2002. Kearns totaled 27 points and 71 penalty minutes in two seasons with the Ice.

Jason Baird shoots on Amarillo goaltender Steve DeBus during a shootout in a game at Conseco Fieldhouse in 2002–03. The Ice modeled special uniforms they wore to celebrate the team's 15th anniversary. Baird totaled 70 points that season and 149 over two years with the club. He was the team's leading scorer in its final season, 2003–04.

Brent Zelenewich makes a save on Colorado's Greg Pankewicz with Ice defenseman Mario Doyon in pursuit during a game in the 2003–04 season. Zelenwich posted a 2.44 goals against average and 17-6-2 record that season. (Courtesy of John Stark.)

Bernie John, who played all five seasons with the CHL Ice, skates past a Colorado Eagles defenseman in one of his final games with the team. John was the face of the Ice during their CHL days. He played more games (301) and totaled more assists (262) and points (353) than anyone in team history. After helping lead the Ice to the 2000 Miron Cup championship, he served the team's final four seasons as captain. He assisted on the final goal in team history, a tally by Jared Dumba with 1:06 left in a 3-1 playoff loss to the Bossier-Shreveport Mudbugs. (Courtesy of John Stark.)

EIGHT
The Coliseum

INDIANA STATE FAIRGROUNDS PEPSI COLISEUM
OPENED: Nov. 1, 1939
FIRST HOCKEY GAME: Nov. 1, 1939 (Indianapolis Capitals 5, Syracuse Stars 1)
LAST PROFESSIONAL GAME: March 28, 2004 (Indianapolis Ice 7, Bossier-Shreveport Mudbugs 4)
CAPACITY: Between 8,200 (present) and 10,500 (late 1940s)
LARGEST CROWD: 10,502: Feb. 16, 1947 (Indianapolis Capitals 2, Hershey Bears 1)
HOME OF: Indianapolis Capitals (AHL) 1939–52; Indianapolis Chiefs (IHL) 1955–62;
Indianapolis Capitols (CPHL) 1963; Indianapolis Checkers (CHL) 1982-84; (IHL) 1984–85;
Indianapolis Ice (IHL) 1988–94, 1998–99; (CHL) 1999–2004.

When Arthur Wirtz brought his hockey team into the brand new $1 million State Fairgrounds Coliseum in 1939, he might have foreseen the game being played into the next century there.

But he probably didn't expect it to outlast every other existing arena in professional hockey. Five different rinks have hosted regular-season home games for Indianapolis' six different hockey teams. None have been a bigger part of the fabric than the Coliseum, which brought hockey to the city in 1939 and continues to play host to the sport in the 21st century.

Of the 50 hockey seasons that have begun in Indianapolis since 1939, the Coliseum—renamed the Pepsi Coliseum during the 1991–92 season—has been the home rink for 37, including all seven championship teams. From its construction and opening November 1, 1939, until its infamous explosion on Halloween 1963, the Coliseum was the only rink in Indianapolis. It played host to 21 season openers in its first 25 years.

Also, many of Indianapolis' youth learned to play hockey and skate on the oversized 210x90-foot ice sheet—10 feet longer and five feet wider than the NHL standard. The first youth hockey leagues were formed in the 1940s, with a big boost from Capitals defenseman Hal Jackson. Two local youth hockey alumni came back to play for the Ice as adults—Mike Stapleton and Casey Harris, whose fathers both played for the Indianapolis Racers.

Stapleton has a very unusual memory of the rink from his younger days. "I broke my collarbone there," he said. "I was running up the stairs, tripped and broke it." More than a decade later, he returned and helped bring the city a championship, leading the Ice to the 1990 Turner Cup title, one that was clinched at the coliseum in front of 6,003 noisy fans with a 2-0 victory over Muskegon.

The Indianapolis Capitals clinched their 1942 and 1950 Calder Cup championships on home ice. Two other titles—the Checkers' 1982 Adams Cup title and the Ice's 1990 Turner Cup championship—were clinched on Coliseum ice. All seven of Indy's championship teams have called it home—the 1958 Chiefs, 1983 Checkers and 2000 Ice all clinched titles on the road.

Noise is one of the Coliseum's main strengths. The one-level seating bowl encircles the ice, while brick and glass-block walls and a pitched roof amplify sound around the building.

"I don't think I've ever heard anything louder than the final game in 1990," former Ice president Ray Compton said. "People were standing on their seats."

It was a place for hockey fans to come together on winter nights—rabid fans who followed hockey teams from the Caps through the Ice in the barn. Crowd sizes fluctuated from over 10,000 in the late 1940s to under 2,000 in 1963. When the Checkers and Ice played there in multiple stints from 1982–2004, attendance usually averaged around 4,000 fans per game.

"The hard core of fans, they followed us all over the place," said Cliff Hicks, who played goal for the Chiefs from 1956-59. "We'd play on a weeknight in Cincinnati or Toledo, they'd follow us and drive back home and go to work the next morning. They were amazing. Even when we won the championship, we didn't have a huge following, but we had an awfully hard-core of fans."

At the time it was built, the Coliseum was considered state-of-the-art. After the Boston Garden, Maple Leaf Gardens, Chicago Stadium, Montreal Forum and Hersheypark Arena were replaced in the 1990s and early 21st century, it became the oldest venue hosting professional hockey in North America.

"The first time I walked into the Coliseum, the first thought I had was, 'The dressing rooms are huge.' Not by today's standards, but compared to the old rinks we used to play in, they were huge. It was a great place to play. It was well-lit, the ice surface was very good, even in warmer weather. The crowds used to stay in the lower level, which made it all the better," said Hicks.

The 1939 construction replaced the original Coliseum, a wooden building that was built in 1907 on the same site and razed in 1938 to make way for the new arena. Many of the events hosted by the original Coliseum would move to the new one.

The Coliseum was built for multipurpose use, befitting its location as the Indiana State Fairgrounds' main indoor venue—its most visible feature to that end is the large distance between the main seating and the rink, in order to allow enough floor space for horse and animal shows during the State Fair. The outer wall—which stretches a few feet beyond the hockey boards — is currently painted white, but it was maroon when the arena was built. Then-Capitals coach Herb Lewis tried to get that changed—saying the dark walls could obscure a goaltender's vision of the puck. They weren't painted white until the mid-1980s.

When the Coliseum hosted its first event—a game between the Indianapolis Capitals and Syracuse Stars on Nov. 1, 1939—it was the second-largest indoor sporting venue in the state, supplanted only by Butler University's 15,000-seat fieldhouse two and a half miles away.

It has hosted some colorful moments. In 1949–50, the Capitals used a quarrel with Pittsburgh to boost them on the way to a 12-game unbeaten streak and an eventual Calder Cup championship. At the time, the team benches were side-by-side on the south side of the rink. But it wasn't as set in stone which team would use which bench and which goal. In a game against the Pittsburgh Hornets, the visitors tried to take the Capitals' usual bench, which was closest to their locker room in the southwest corner of the building. The teams fought, but the matter was restored and the angry Capitals won 5-4. A new visitors' bench was built opposite the Caps' bench on the north side of the rink, where the penalty boxes currently sit.

The rink's biggest crowds came in the 1947–48 season, when an average of 8,133 fans supported the Capitals. In addition to farm shows, hockey games and State Fair activities, presidents John F. Kennedy and George W. Bush have spoken there. Evangelist Billy Graham once hosted a crusade within its walls. And bands as diverse as the Beatles and Supremes have held concerts at the Coliseum.

The Capitals left in 1952 amid declining attendance and a quarrel between Wirtz and the Coliseum's owners over rent. Coliseum Corporation president Mel Ross brought a hockey team into the building three years later, which was called the Chiefs. In that time, the rink also hosted a handful of home games for the National Basketball Association's Cincinnati Royals.

On October 31, 1963, the building's defining moment came during an Ice Follies show. Propane gas used to heat popcorn leaked from a concession stand. The resulting explosion threw large chunks of concrete into the air and killed 63 people, and the ice rink was used as a temporary morgue. That grisly day closed the Coliseum for a short time. All gas lines were taken out of the building. The Indianapolis Capitols moved to Cincinnati.

The building was given new life in 1967 when the American Basketball Association's Indiana Pacers came into being and began a seven-year run of playing to sold-out houses. They won three ABA titles in that span. It would host hockey a generation later, as the Indianapolis Checkers moved to the Coliseum in 1981 and won two championships in their first two seasons there. The Indianapolis Ice called the Coliseum home in 12 of their 16 seasons.

The arena underwent a renovation after the 1963 explosion that—among other things—led to new scoreboards being placed on each side. They were replaced with identical, newer scoreboards in 1990. The rink was given a new name in 1991, when Pepsi bought the naming rights, making it the Pepsi Coliseum. It underwent a major renovation starting with the Ice's return in 1998, with nearly all of the seats being replaced—many being taken from the RCA Dome, which was undergoing a major renovation of its own. An air-conditioning system was put into place, the home locker room in the southwest corner was expanded and the concourses remodeled, giving the rink a new life for the 21st century, where it will likely remain the home of local hockey.

The Coliseum as it looked in 2004. It has undergone minor face lifts, but the exterior and interior remain very similar to 1939, when the building opened. In 2002, the rink became the oldest active building in the country to host professional hockey. The main entrance is on the north side and faces the Indiana State Fairgrounds' main parking areas.

The interior of the Coliseum in 2004, during a game between the Indianapolis Ice and Colorado Eagles. (Courtesy of John Stark.)

The interior of the old Fairgrounds Coliseum, which was built in 1907 and razed in 1938 to make way for the new building, is seen here. It never hosted hockey, but many of the events it hosted eventually moved over to the new building when it was finished on the same site. (Courtesy of the Indiana State Faigrounds.)

Pictured is the erection of the first steel beams to hold up the sides of what would become the Fairgrounds Coliseum in early 1939. (Courtesy of the Indiana State Fairgrounds.)

The Coliseum's construction as seen from the inside on June 17, 1939. The exposed steel beams that provide much of the building's shape are visible at the top of the photograph. The outline of the seating bowl is beginning to take shape, with the lower-level box seats in place on one side of the rink. (Courtesy of the Indiana State Fairgrounds.)

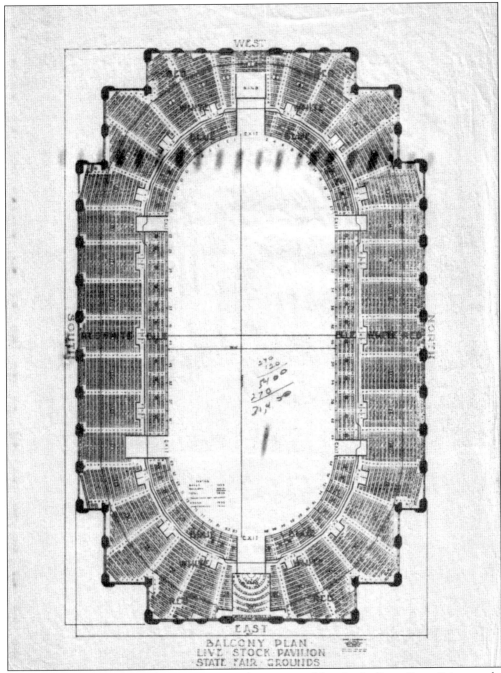

A 1959 revision of the Coliseum's seating chart, as used by the Indiana State Fairgrounds. (Courtesy of the Indiana State Fairgrounds.)

The shell of the Fairgrounds Coliseum from the exterior May 17, 1939. The steel beams are in place. The building is only a shell as of this photograph, but it would play host to its first game six months later. (Courtesy of the Indiana State Fairgrounds.)

Workers touch up the Coliseum's ice rink. (Courtesy of the Indiana State Fairgrounds.)

The Coliseum is beginning to take shape August 15, 1939, less than three months before the first event. The limestone face over the main entrance is in place, as are the glass-block windows that surround the building. (Courtesy of the Indiana State Fairgrounds.)

The first thing fans see when they enter the Coliseum—the ticket booths that line the northern entrance of the building.

Here is the inside of the Coliseum as it looked in the 1960s, with the hockey rink back in place. Notice there is no glass above the boards. The scoreboards, which were used from the 1960s to the 1990s, have been installed. They were replaced in the early 1990s with identically-sized models. (Courtesy of the Indiana State Faigrounds.)

The Coliseum has been about much more than hockey games in its tenure. It is a key venue on the Indiana State Fairgrounds, as evidenced here by this 1953 4-H photo. The building has also hosted concerts by major acts ranging from the Beatles to the Supremes to Andy Griffith, visits by evangelist Billy Graham, speeches by United States presidents John F. Kennedy and George W. Bush, and annual events such as the Boat, Sport and Travel Show. Notice the scoreboard hanging above the floor, which is the one used when the Capitals played there. The game clock is the large dial in the middle, with smaller penalty clocks flanking it. (Courtesy of the Indiana State Fairgrounds.)

The cornerstone of the Fairgrounds Coliseum was placed in 1939. The building has two identical cornerstones, one on each end of the main entrance.

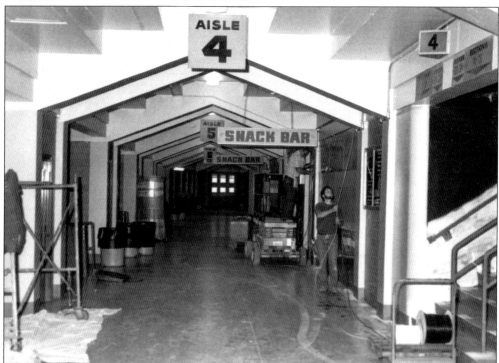

Renovations were made to the Coliseum's concourse in 1988, before the Ice moved in. (Courtesy of the Indiana State Fairgrounds.)

NINE

Other Homes

MARKET SQUARE ARENA
OPENED: September, 1974 (Glen Campbell concert)
FIRST REGULAR-SEASON HOCKEY GAME: Oct. 17, 1974 (Michigan Stags 4, Indianapolis Racers 2)
LAST HOCKEY GAME: March 20, 1999 (Las Vegas Thunder 5, Indianapolis Ice 2)
CAPACITY: Listed between 15,860 and 16,040 for hockey
LARGEST CROWD: 16,040, April 3, 1976 (New England Whalers 5, Indianapolis Racers 2);
April 29, 1976 (Playoffs: New England Whalers 6, Indianapolis Racers 0); April 16, 1977
(Playoffs: Indianapolis Racers 3, Cincinnati Stingers 1)
IMPLODED: July 8, 2001
HOME OF: Indianapolis Racers (WHA) 1974–78; Indianapolis Checkers (CHL) 1979–81;
(IHL) 1985–87 (also hosted two playoff games 1983, one playoff game 1985); Indianapolis Ice
(IHL) 1994–98 (eight games 1998–99, three playoff games 1993).

Market Square Arena is fondly remembered by many Indianapolis-area hockey fans for bringing the city big-league hockey for four and a half years in the wild 1970s.

A perfectly-shaped building for hockey, all of its seats were built to center around the rink, with most of them sloping up the two sides. The rink itself was suspended three stories above Market Street. The fans often climbed up six flights of stairs to get to their seats.

When MSA opened in 1974, it ushered in a new era for the sport in Indianapolis, which hadn't played host to a professional hockey game in 11 years.

The Indianapolis Racers lasted only four and a half years, but they left plenty of memories— the two biggest being their 1977 playoff sweep of the Cincinnati Stingers and Wayne Gretzky's eight-game stint as a Racers center, where he began his record-setting career as a 17-year-old. It sold all 16,040 seats for the first time April 3, 1976, for a game against the New England Whalers. It did so three weeks later for Game 7 of the Racers-Whalers playoff series, which New England won 6-0. The only other Racers-era sellout came in 1977, when the Racers clinched a four-game sweep of the Cincinnati Stingers in the opening round of the playoffs.

After the Racers folded, MSA was an off-and-on home of the Indianapolis Checkers and Ice, hosting the Checkers for a pair of two-year stints and the Ice full-time for four years and part-time for two others. The Checkers set a minor-league record crowd of 15,925 there on March 7, 1981. The Ice filled it multiple times during their annual Pack the House Nights.

MSA was a multipurpose arena that was Indianapolis' main indoor venue from the time it opened until it closed in 1999, hosting not only hockey, but the Indiana Pacers of the ABA and NBA, and multiple concerts. Elvis Presley played his final concert there in 1977—which was memorialized near the sixth-floor ticket booths. Its demise came when the Indiana Pacers—who had been tenants since the building opened in 1974—lobbied the city to build Conseco Fieldhouse. When the new arena went up, MSA was shuttered and eventually imploded.

The final hockey game was played on March 20, 1999. The Ice were playing the last of eight home games at MSA, and wore replica Racers uniforms for their game against the Las Vegas Thunder. The Ice lost 5-2, but with Bob Lamey emceeing the evening and former Racers Peter Driscoll and Michel Dion on hand—not to mention a video greeting from Wayne Gretzky—the evening turned out to be a festive one. The Ice went on to finish their season at the Coliseum and moved down the street with the Pacers for their new part-time home.

CONSECO FIELDHOUSE
OPENED: Nov. 6, 1999 (NBA basketball: Indiana Pacers vs. Boston Celtics)
FIRST HOCKEY GAME: Nov. 20, 1999 (Indianapolis Ice 4, San Antonio Iguanas 1)
CAPACITY: approx. 15,000 for hockey
LARGEST HOCKEY CROWD: 14,739, March 1, 2003 (Memphis RiverKings 5, Indianapolis Ice 2)
HOME OF: Indianapolis Ice (CHL) part-time 1999–2004

Conseco Fieldhouse opened in 1999 as an indoor arena's answer to baseball's Camden Yards—a new building put together with old-style architectural features in mind—most obviously seen in the barrel-vault roof, the large windows that overlook the playing surface and the massive quantities of brick and exposed steel hovering above the seating bowl.

The building was most obviously built for basketball—the hockey rink is offset into one end of the arena, where fans in the upper-deck seats cannot see one of the goals. But it has been well-received by both the Ice and local fans, who come in large numbers when the Ice visit. The Ice have played between four and six games per year there, one of which is designated Pack the House Night. In four of the Ice's five seasons, more than 14,000 fans showed up for Pack the House Night, including a CHL-record 14,739 on March 1, 2003.

Players described the rink as the best in the Central Hockey League. "This is an NHL building," said longtime Ice captain Bernie John, who played in every one of the Ice's games at the Fieldhouse.

The building's primary tenant is the Indiana Pacers, who advanced to the NBA Finals in their first year in the building and routinely sold all 18,345 seats. The WNBA's Indiana Fever and Arena Football League's Indiana Firebirds have also called the building home. Conseco Fieldhouse has also brought several first-class events to the city, hosting the World Basketball Championships, the Big Ten men's and women's basketball tournaments, several major concerts and even the World Short-Course Swimming Championships, which were held in a temporary pool.

CINCINNATI GARDENS (CAPACITY 11,000)
Faced with flagging attendance at home, the Indianapolis Chiefs decided to play a handful of home games in the Cincinnati Gardens during the 1959–60 season—a year after the IHL dynasty Cincinnati Mohawks folded.

The Gardens was built in 1948 and had its first event in early 1949—a decade after the Coliseum—using a similar seating plan to Toronto's Maple Leaf Gardens. The Chiefs played their first game there Jan. 10, 1960, against the St. Paul Saints, a game the Saints won 5-2. But it didn't count in the standings—the Chiefs launched, and won, a protest of the game's outcome. The Chiefs played two other games there in 1960—a 4-3 victory over Minneapolis January 24 and a 7-0 win over the Fort Wayne Komets February 7. The Chiefs often moved games to Cincinnati when they had a home game the night before, instead of trying to draw the same crowd on consecutive days.

The Chiefs played many games there as a visiting team, including the 1957 Turner Cup Finals, which the host Cincinnati Mohawks swept. Four decades later, the Indianapolis Ice and Cincinnati Cyclones would play a number of games against each other there. In 1963, another Indianapolis team called the Gardens home, when the Indianapolis Capitols were forced to move following the October 31 explosion at the Fairgrounds Coliseum. The team moved to the Gardens and played the balance of the season as the Cincinnati Wings.

CARMEL ICE SKADIUM (CAPACITY 1,000)
The old Central Hockey League's 21-year run from 1963 to 1984 ended with one of its longest-standing members, the Tulsa Oilers, skating away with the final Adams Cup championship. But they did so without a home, and hoisted the trophy in front of a packed house in a rink that had never been built to host professional games.

The journey there was an odd one befitting a five-team league on the verge of collapse. The Oilers had been locked out of their arena at mid-season and taken over by the league. They finished their schedule on the road. Both they and the Indianapolis Checkers pulled upsets in first-round playoff series—the Checkers beating the highly-favored Colorado Flames, and the nomadic Oilers knocking off the Salt Lake Golden Eagles.

With the Oilers having no home ice, the entire Adams Cup final series was slated to be played in Indianapolis. The Oilers—as they were known after losing their city—swept through the first three games, but a problem arose when the Coliseum was unavailable for Game 4. The Checkers and CHL scrambled and decided to play the game at Carmel. Oiler Mike Backman scored 35 seconds into the game, setting the stage for a 3-2 Oiler victory and potentially the most unusual championship celebration site in hockey.

The Ice Skadium has largely hosted recreational skating and youth hockey. Its seating is nine rows of wooden bleachers spanning the west side of the main rink.

The Conseco Fieldhouse is where the Ice have played between four and six games per year since the 1999–2000 season.

Here is the inside of Conseco Fieldhouse and its seating chart for hockey. The arena was built with basketball as its No. 1 option, so the hockey rink is off-center. (Courtesy of the Indianapolis Ice.)

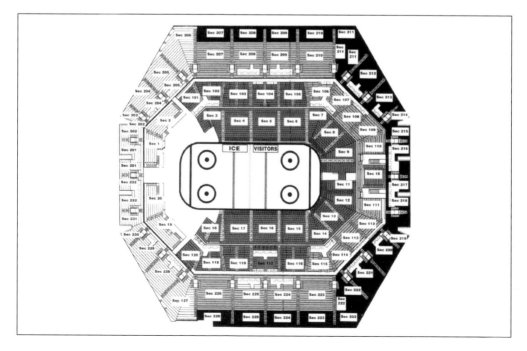

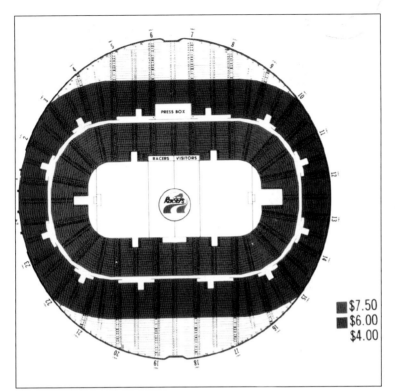

$7.50
$6.00
$4.00

Market Square Arena was most often filled during the Indianapolis Racers' tenure. The Racers sold all 16,040 seats on three occasions, including two playoff games in 1976 and 1977. The seating bowl itself was circular, with seats concentrated on the sides of the rink. (Indianapolis Racers.)

The Indianapolis Ice skate across the rink at Market Square Arena during its final hockey game on March 20, 1999.

Remi Royer of the Ice fights Sami Helenius of the Las Vegas Thunder during the final hockey game at Market Square Arena. The rink's design put fans on top of the action all the way around.

The Carmel Ice Skadium played host to the final hockey game ever played in the original Central Hockey League, a matchup between the Indianapolis Checkers and the former Tulsa Oilers, a team without a home rink. Because all of the other rinks in Indianapolis were booked, Game 4 of the 1984 Adams Cup Finals was played here. The Oilers clinched the championship that evening.

Appendix

RECORDS AND STATISTICS

THE CHAMPIONS

1941–42 Capitals (AHL Calder Cup): Dick Behling, Connie Brown, Les Douglas, Joe Fisher, Gus Giesebrecht, Hal Jackson, Bill Jennings, Jack Keating, Hec Kilrea, Ken Kilrea, Jud McAtee, Doug McCaig, Sandy Ross, Joe Sawyer, Joe Turner, Herb Lewis (coach), Dick Miller (general manager), Arthur Wirtz (owner).

1949–50 Capitals (AHL Calder Cup): Al Dewsbury, Fred Glover, Gordon Haidy, Ott Heller (player/coach), Joe Lund, Pat Lundy, Doug McKay, Don Morrison, Rod Morrison, Nels Podolsky, Max Quackenbush, Clare Raglan, Jerry Reid, Terry Sawchuk, Enio Scilisizzi, James Uniac, Lyall Wiseman, Benny Woit, Arthur Wirtz (owner).

1957–58 Chiefs (IHL Turner Cup): Marc Boileau, Bob Bowness, Pierre Brillant, Don Busch, Sam Gregory, Cliff Hicks, Frank Kuzma, Germain "Red" Leger, Lloyd McKay, Ron Morgan, Bill Short, Myron Stankiewicz, Alex Viskelis, Ken Willey, Leo Lamoreaux (coach), Mel Ross (owner/general manager).

1981–82 Checkers (CHL Adams Cup): Bruce Affleck, Bruce Andres, Frank Beaton, Kelly Davis, Kevin Devine, Glen Duncan, Mats Hallin, Neil Hawryliw, Mike Hordy, Randy Johnston, Red Laurence, Tim Lockridge, Garth MacGuigan, Darcy Regier, Dave Simpson, Charlie Skjodt, Lorne Stamler, Steve Stoyanovich, Monty Trottier, Rob Holland, Kelly Hrudey, Fred Creighton (coach/GM).

1982–83 Checkers (CHL Adams Cup): Bruce Affleck, Neal Coulter, Kelly Davis, Kevin Devine, Gord Dineen, Glen Duncan, Mike Greeder, Ron Handy, Dave Hanson, Rob Holland, Scott Howson, Kelly Hrudey, Randy Johnston, Red Laurence, Tim Lockridge, Garth MacGuigan, Darcy Regier, Dave Simpson, Lorne Stamler, Steve Stoyanovich, Monty Trottier, Fred Creighton (coach/GM).

1989–90 Ice (IHL Turner Cup): Dave Bassegio, Bob Bassen, Bruce Cassidy, Craig Channell, Mike Eagles, Jim Johannson, Ryan McGill, Mike McNeill, Brian Noonan, Darren Pang, Mike Peluso, Guy Phillips, Jim Playfair, Warren Rychel, Mike Rucinski, Cam Russell, Mike Stapleton, Jari Torkki, Jim Waite, Sean Williams, Darryl Sutter (coach), Ray Compton (general manager), Horn Chen (owner).

1999–2000 Ice (CHL Miron Cup): Mike Berger, Ken Boone, Yvan Corbin, Dan Cousineau, Rob Davidson, Blaz Emersic, Jan Jas, Peter Jas, Bernie John, Lubos Krajcovic, Eric Landry, Chris MacKenzie, Jamie Morris, Sebastian Pajerski, Arvid Rekis, Taj Schaffnit, Benoit Thibert, Mike Torkoff, Daniel Villeneuve, Corey Waring, Rod Davidson (coach), Joe Trotta (assistant coach), Brad Beery (general manager), Gary Pedigo, Jim Hallet, Ed Russell, Tom Zupancic (owners).

INDIANAPOLIS CAPITALS (AHL 1939–52)
YEAR-BY-YEAR RECORD

YEAR	RECORD	PLACE	LEADING SCORER (G-A-P)	PLAYOFFS
1939–40	26-20-10	1/5 IAHL West	Bill Hudson (27-27-54)	2-3 (lost semifinal)
1940–41	17-28-11	4/5 AHL West	Connie Brown (16-28-44)	none
1941–42	34-15-7	1/5 AHL West	Connie Brown (19-34-53)	6-4 (Calder Cup Champs)
1942–43	29-23-4	3/8 AHL	Adam Brown (34-51-85)	4-3 (lost final)
1943–44	20-18-16	2/3 AHL West	Bill Thomson (20-38-58)	1-4 (lost semifinal)
1944–45	25-24-11	2/4 AHL West	Pete Leswick (29-39-68)	1-4 (lost semifinal)
1945–46	33-20-9	1/4 AHL West	Les Douglas (44-46-90)	1-4 (lost semifinal)
1946–47	33-18-13	4/5 AHL West	Les Douglas (26-57-83)	none
1947–48	32-30-6	4/5 AHL West	Cliff Simpson (48-62-110)	none
1948–49	39-17-12	2/5 AHL West	Fred Glover (35-48-83)	0-2 (lost 1st round)
1949–50	35-24-11	2/5 AHL West	Pat Lundy (30-47-77)	8-0 (Calder Cup Champs)
1950–51	38-29-3	2/5 AHL West	Fred Glover (48-36-84)	0-2 (lost 1st round)
1951–52	22-40-6	5/5 AHL West	Earl Reibel (33-34-67)	none

COACHES		RECORD (PLAYOFFS)	NOTABLE
1939–43	Herb Lewis	106-86-32 (12-10)	2 division titles, 1942 Calder Cup title
1943	Carson Cooper	1-0-2	Fill-in until Sorrell could arrive
1943–46	John Sorrell	62-55-30 (2-8)	Moved into front office mid-season 1946
1946	Earl Seibert	15-7-4 (1-4)	Division champs in half-season
1946–47	Tommy Ivan	33-18-13	Only non-playing coach in Caps history
1947–48	Johnny Mowers	32-30-6	Also played goal for the Caps
1948–52	Ott Heller	134-110-32 (8-4)	1950 Calder Cup champs

CAREER RECORDS

GAMES

Rod Morrison	319	1943–44, 1946–51
Enio Scilisizzi	314	1946–52
Nels Podolsky	264	1946–51

GOALS

Cliff Simpson	136	1942–43, 1945–49
Enio Scilisizzi	125	1946–52
Fred Glover	110	1948–52

POINTS

Cliff Simpson	281	1942–43, 1945–49
Enio Scilisizzi	280	1946–52
Les Douglas	268	1940–43, 1945–47

GOALTENDING WINS

Terry Sawchuk	67	1948–50
Ralph Almas	64	1946–48
Jim Henry	37	1950–51

GOALS AGAINST AVERAGE

Joe Turner	2.44	1941–42
Harry Lumley	2.64	1943–45
Jimmy Franks	2.66	1939–41

INDIANAPOLIS CHIEFS (IHL 1955–62)
YEAR-BY-YEAR RECORD

YEAR	RECORD	PLACE	LEADING SCORER (G-A-P)	PLAYOFFS
1955–56	11-48-1	6/6 IHL	Maurice Lamirande (17-23-40)	none
1956–57	26-29-5	2/6 IHL	Pierre Brillant (38-41-79)	(3-5) L final
1957–58	28-30-6	4/6 IHL	Marc Boileau (26-61-87)	(7-4) Turner Cup champs
1958–59	26-30-4	4/5 IHL	Pierre Brillant (57-41-98)	(1-4) L semifinal
1959–60	25-40-3	4/4 IHL East	Pierre Brillant (50-37-87)	none
1960–61	20-46-4	4/4 IHL East	Russ McClegnahan (23-64-87)	none
1961–62	19-49-0	6/7 IHL	Bobby Rivard (40-51-91)	none

COACHES	RECORD (PLAYOFFS)	NOTABLE
1955–56 John Sorrell	5-29-0	Moved to general manager Jan. 4, 1956.
1956–58, 60 Leo Lamoureux	63-83-12	Won Turner Cup 1958
1958–59 Max Silverman	26-30-4	
1959–60 Marcel Clements	25-40-3	
1960 Laurin/Short	1-8-0	Interim coaches after Lamoureux became ill
1960–61 Ab DeMarco	15-34-4	Finished 1960–61 season
1961–62 Alex Shibicky	19-49-0	

CAREER RECORDS

GAMES
Pierre Brillant	278	1956–61
Billy Short	238	1957–61
Lloyd McKey	219	1956–61

GOALS
Pierre Brillant	204	1956–61
Germain Leger	61	1957–60
Hank Therrien	57	1959–62

POINTS
Pierre Brillant	355	1956–61
Billy Short	153	1957–61
Germain Leger	147	1957–60

GOALTENDING WINS
Cliff Hicks	82	1956–60
Chuck Adamson	41	1959–61
Carl Wetzel	15	1960–61

GOALS AGAINST AVERAGE
Cliff Hicks	3.58	1956–60
Carl Wetzel	3.83	1960–61
Chuck Adamson	5.00	1959–61

Indianapolis Capitols (CPHL 1963)

YEAR	RECORD	PLACE	LEADING SCORER (G-A-P)	PLAYOFFS
1963	1-7-1	DNF	Don Chiz (5-1-6)	

*Did not finish season in Indianapolis due to Oct. 31, 1963 explosion at the Fairgrounds Coliseum. Team moved to Cincinnati Nov. 7, 1963.

INDIANAPOLIS RACERS (WHA 1974–78)
YEAR-BY-YEAR RECORD

YEAR	RECORD	PLACE	LEADING SCORER (G-A-P)	PLAYOFFS
1974–75	18-57-3	4/4 WHA East	Bob Whitlock (31-26-57)	none
1975–76	35-39-6	1/4 WHA East	Pat Stapleton (5-40-45)	(3-4) L semifinal
1976–77	36-37-8	3/6 WHA East	Darryl Maggs (16-55-71)	(5-4) L div. final
1977–78	24-51-5	8/8 WHA	Claude St. Sauveur (36-42-78)	none
1978	5-18-2	DNF	Blaine Stoughton (9-9-18)	Folded 12/15
			Don Larway (8-10-18)	

COACHES		RECORD (PLAYOFFS)	NOTABLE
1974–75	Gerry Moore	19-61-3	Fired five games into 1975–76 season.
1975–77	Jacques Demers	70-72-14 (8-8)	Led Racers to only two playoff appearances.
1977–78	Ron Ingram	16-31-4	Fired with 29 games to go in 1977–78 season.
1978	Bill Goldsworthy	8-20-1	Player-coach, finished 1977–78 season.
1978	Pat Stapleton	5-18-2	Team folded midway through season.

CAREER RECORDS

GAMES

Ken Block	267	1974–78
Reggie Thomas	208	1975–78
Bob Sicinski	207	1974–77

GOALS

Reggie Thomas	63	1975–78
Rene LeClerc	60	1975–78
Blair McDonald	53	1974–77

POINTS

Michel Parizeau	136	1975–78
Rene LeClerc	133	1975–78
Bob Sicinski	132	1974–77

GOALTENDING WINS

Michel Dion	31	1975–77
Andy Brown	23	1974–77
Jim Park	20	1975–78

GOALS AGAINST AVERAGE

Michel Dion	3.08	1975–77
Jim Park	3.70	1975–78
Andy Brown	3.94	1974–77

INDIANAPOLIS CHECKERS (CHL 1979–84; IHL 1985–87)
YEAR-BY-YEAR RECORD

YEAR	RECORD	PLACE	LEADING SCORER (G-A-P)	PLAYOFFS
1979–80	40-32-7	2/9 CHL	Alex McKendry (40-37-77)	(4-3) L semifinal
1980–81	44-30-6	3/9 CHL	Neil Hawryliw (37-42-79)	(2-3) L 1st round
1981–82	42-33-5	3/5 CHL North	Red Laurence (43-55-98)	(11-2) Adams Cup champ
1982–83	50-28-2	1/6 CHL	Red Laurence (43-55-98)	(9-4) Adams Cup champ
1983–84	36-34-2	4/5 CHL	Red Laurence (41-37-78)	(4-6) L final
1984–85	31-44-4-3	4/4 IHL West	Charlie Skjodt (33-34-67)	(3-4) L 1st round
1985–86	41-35-1-5	5/5 IHL West	Charlie Skjodt (30-65-95)	(1-4) L 1st round
1986–87	37-38-0-7	4/4 IHL West	Ron Handy (55-80-135)	(2-4) L 1st round

COACHES	RECORD (PLAYOFFS)	NOTABLE
CHL		
1979–81 Bert Marshall	84-62-13 (6-6)	
1981–84 Fred Creighton	128-95-9 (24-12)	2 Adams Cup championships
IHL		
1984–85 Darcy Regier	27-36-4-3	Fired 3/2April 85
1985 Fred Creighton	1-0-0-0 (3-3)	Interim 1 game 3/26/85. Coached balance of playoffs.
1985 Moe Bartoli	4-8-0-0 (0-1)	Fired after 1st playoff game, replaced by Creighton.
1985–87 Ron Ullyot	78-73-1-12 (3-8)	

CHL CAREER RECORDS

GAMES

Kevin Devine	388	1979–84
Garth MacGuigan	385	1979–84
Darcy Regier	377	1979–84

GOALS

Garth MacGuigan	151	1979–84
Red Laurence	127	1981–84
Kevin Devine	123	1979–84

POINTS

Garth MacGuigan	350	1979–84
Red Laurence	274	1981–84
Kevin Devine	259	1979–84

GOALTENDING WINS

Rob Holland	59	1980–84
Kelly Hrudey	56	1981–84
Roland Melanson	31	1980–81

GOALS AGAINST AVERAGE

Roland Melanson	2.57	1980–81
Richard Brodeur	2.88	1979–80
Kelly Hrudey	3.02	1981–84

IHL CAREER RECORDS

GAMES

Marc Magnan	218	1984–87
Bob Lakso	213	1984–87
Charlie Skjodt	151	1984–86

GOALS

Bob Lakso	106	1984–87
Charlie Skjodt	61	1984–86
Ron Handy	55	1986–87

POINTS

Bob Lakso	228	1984–87
Charlie Skjodt	160	1984–87
Ron Handy	135	1986–87

GOALTENDING WINS

Rob Holland	42	1984–86
Mike Zanier	29	1985–87
Dave Parro	16	1986–87

GOALS AGAINST AVERAGE

Rob Holland	3.54	1984–86
Mike Zanier	3.58	1985–87
Dave Parro	4.18	1986–87

Indianapolis Ice (IHL 1988–99)
Year-by-Year Record

Year	Record	Place	Leading Scorer (G-A-P)	Playoffs
1988–89	26-54-2	5/5 IHL West	Ron Handy (43-57-100)	none
1989–90	53-21-8	1/5 IHL West	Brian Noonan (40-36-76)	(12-2) Turner Cup champs
1990–91	48-29-5	2/4 IHL East	Sean Williams (46-52-98)	(3-4) L Div. semifinal
1991–92	31-41-10	5/5 IHL East	Sean Williams (29-36-65)	none
1992–93	34-39-9	2/3 IHL Atlantic	Tony Hrkac (45-87-132)	(1-4) L Conf. semifinal
1993–94	28-46-7	3/3 IHL Atlantic	Rob Cimetta (26-54-80)	none
1994–95	32-41-8	4/4 IHL Central	Craig Fisher (53-40-93)	none
1995–96	43-33-6	2/4 IHL Central	Kip Miller (32-59-91)	(2-3) L Conf. quarterfinal
1996–97	44-29-9	1/4 IHL Central	Brad Werenka (20-56-76)	(1-3) L Conf. quarterfinal
1997–98	40-36-6	3/5 IHL Central	Todd White (46-36-82)	(2-3) L Conf. quarterfinal
1998–99	33-37-12	3/4 IHL Central	Dave Hymovitz (46-30-76)	(3-4) L Conf. semifinal

Coaches		Record (Playoffs)	Notable
1988–89	Archie Henderson	18-35-1	Left team after being diagnosed with colon cancer.
1989	Ron Handy	0-2-0	Emergency coach after Henderson left.
1989	Reggie Thomas	8-17-1	Replaced Henderson to finish season
1989–90	Darryl Sutter	53-21-8 (12-2)	West Division, Turner Cup champs in only year
1990–91	Dave McDowall	48-29-5 (3-4)	Dropped playoff heartbreaker in seventh-game OT.
1991–93	John Marks	59-75-14	Replaced with 16 games to go in 1992–93 season.
1993–95	Duane Sutter	66-92-20 (1-4)	Replaced Marks to finish 1992–93 season.
1995–98	Bob Ferguson	127-98-21 (5-9)	Won 1997 Central Division title.
1998–99	Bruce Cassidy	33-37-12 (3-4)	Led Ice to 1st playoff series win since 1990.

Career Records

Games

Sean Williams	320	1989–93
Ivan Droppa	297	1992–97
Rob Conn	268	1991–95, 1996–97

Goals

Sean Williams	130	1989–93
Brian Noonan	107	1989–91, 1998–99
Rob Conn	77	1991–95, 1996–97

Points

Sean Williams	286	1989–93
Brian Noonan	233	1989–91, 1998–99
Steve Dubinsky	155	1995–97

Goaltending Wins

Jim Waite	116	1989–92, 1994–97
Ray LeBlanc	54	1989–94
Marc Lamothe	45	1996–99

Goals Against Average

Dominik Hasek	2.91	1990–92
Marc Lamothe	2.94	1996–99
Jim Waite	3.13	1989–92, 1994–97

126

INDIANAPOLIS ICE (CHL 1999–2004)
YEAR-BY-YEAR RECORD

YEAR	RECORD	PLACE	LEADING SCORER (G-A-P)	PLAYOFFS
1999–00	39-28-3	2/6 CHL West	Yvan Corbin (62-65-127) (10-5)	Miron Cup champs
			Chris MacKenzie (47-80-127)	
2000–01	31-32-7	4/6 CHL East	Yvan Corbin (75-54-129)	(0-3) L Div. semifinal
2001–02	20-37-7	4/4 CHL Northeast	Peter Bournazakis (29-48-77)	none
2002–03	39-16-9	1/4 CHL Northeast	Kevin St. Jacques (22-56-78)	(3-5) L Conf. final
2003–04	37-23-4	2/4 CHL Northeast	Jason Baird (27-52-79)	(2-3) L Conf. semifinal

COACHES		RECORD (PLAYOFFS)	NOTABLE
1999–02	Rod Davidson	90-97-17 (10-8)	2000 Miron Cup champs
2002–04	Ken McRae	76-39-13 (5-8)	2003 Northeast division champs

CAREER RECORDS

GAMES
Bernie John	301	1999–2004
Dan Cousineau	192	1999–2002
Ryan Aikia	180	2001–04

GOALS
Yvan Corbin	131	1999–2001
Bernie John	91	1999–2004
Chris MacKenzie	88	1999–2002

POINTS
Bernie John	351	1999–2004
Chris MacKenzie	297	1999–2002
Yvan Corbin	256	1999–2001

GOALTENDING WINS
Jamie Morris	52	1999–2003
Shawn Silver	29	2002–03
Benoit Thibert	27	1999–2000

GOALS AGAINST AVERAGE
Shawn Silver	2.21	2002–03
Brent Zelenewich	2.44	2003–04
Jeff Sanger	2.85	2003–04

All-time Indianapolis Hockey Career Record Holders

Games

Kevin Devine	542	Racers 1977–78, Checkers 1979–85
Garth MacGuigan	452	Checkers 1979–85
Tim Lockridge	393	Checkers 1979–86
Darcy Regier	377	Checkers 1979–84
Charlie Skjodt	365	Checkers 1979–82, 1984–86
Sean Williams	320	Ice 1989–93
Rod Morrison	319	Capitals 1943–44, 1946–51
Enio Scilisizzi	314	Capitals 1946–51
Bernie John	301	Ice 1999–2004
Ivan Droppa	279	Ice 1992–97

Points

Garth MacGuigan	410	Checkers 1979–85
Charlie Skjodt	376	Checkers 1979–82, 1984–86
Pierre Brillant	365	Chiefs 1956–61
Kevin Devine	352	Racers 1977–78, Checkers 1978–85
Bernie John	353	Ice 1999–2004
Ron Handy	319	Checkers 1982–84, 1986–87, Ice 1988–89
Bob Lakso	300	Checkers 1984–87, Ice 1988–89
Chris MacKenzie	297	Ice 1999–2002
Sean Williams	286	Ice 1989–1993
Cliff Simpson	281	Capitals 1942–43, 1945–49

Goals

Pierre Brillant	204	Chiefs 1956–61
Garth MacGuigan	179	Checkers 1979–85
Kevin Devine	158	Racers 1977–78, Checkers 1979–85
Charlie Skjodt	148	Checkers 1979–82, 1984–86
Bob Lakso	144	Checkers 1984–86, Ice 1988–89

Assists

Bernie John	262	Ice 1999–2004
Garth MacGuigan	231	Checkers 1979–85
Charlie Skjodt	228	Checkers 1979–82, 1984–86
Chris MacKenzie	209	Ice 1999–2002
Kevin Devine	194	Racers 1977–78, Checkers 1979–85

Penalty Minutes

Kevin Devine	1,249	Racers 1977–78, Checkers 1979–85
Marc Magnan	876	Checkers 1984–87
Ken Boone	743	Ice 1999–2001, 2003–04
Warren Rychel	712	Ice 1989–91
Steve McLaren	687	Ice 1995–98